Somebody stole the CORNBREAD from My DRESSING

A Hilarious Comparison Between the
North and South Through Recipes and Recollections

Elizabeth Gourlay Heiskell & Susanne Young Reed

The Overmountain Press
JOHNSON CITY, TENNESSEE

Photography Credits

Sarah Book • sarah K's studio: 32, 120 top
  www.sarahksstudio.com
Courtesy Elizabeth Heiskell: 17 top, 118
Cal Hodges: 120 bottom
Courtesy Susanne Reed: 17 bottom
Stock: 117
Caroline Allison: All others
  www.carolineallison.com

Cover Design

Bill May, Jr. • Stellar Studios
www.stellarstudios.com

Published by

The Overmountain Press
P.O. Box 1261
Johnson City, TN 37605
www.overmountainpress.com

For information about corporate sales,
premiums, and special sales, please contact
The Overmountain Press
by phone at 800-992-2691 or
by e-mail at beth@overmtn.com

Dedication
To Our Families

For Luke and the girls — Stott, Mary Paxton, and Lucia.
The only thing I must do to be reminded of how
God has blessed me is to look into your eyes.
Your encouragement, love, and support made this possible.

Elizabeth

To Charles and Carter, the two loves of my life.
I thank God every day for the two of you.

Susanne

Contents

Lawd, Where Should We Even Begin?

Table of Contents, n.: List of chapters that showcase what will be in the book, or in this case, a mouthwatering appetizer to gourmet Southern traditions.

Foreword
CAROL PUCKETT

The hamlet of Rosedale, Mississippi, is tucked behind an earthen levee, a humble and paltry defense against the mighty Mississippi River. Standing on top of the levee, the earth is pancake flat as far as the eye can see. This is the Mississippi Delta — the most fertile soil in the world deposited by the river that long ago covered this land.

To the west is the river. To the east, a vast expanse of black earth gathers into neat furrowed rows, drawing the eye to the horizon as they narrow to a distant point. These are the farms or plantations, large tracts of land under cultivation. There was a time when cotton was the undisputed king, but today one will more likely find a mix of cotton, soybeans, even corn. The liquid sunsets over the flat land and endless horizon add an even more dreamlike quality to the haunting landscape.

Two young girls play in the shadow of the levee, quiet tree-lined streets their playground. The soothing hum of small-town life is pierced only by the thundering bass horn of tugboats pushing their barges downriver past the port of Rosedale.

Susanne Young Reed and Elizabeth Gourlay Heiskell cemented their lifelong friendship in this small river town in the Mississippi Delta, a region known for its rich and colorful tradition of storytellers, writers, painters, musicians, legendary cooks, and women distinguished in the art of entertaining.

As small children, Susanne, daughter of a beloved high school football coach whose penchant for winning championships and sending his small-town players to the pros was well-known, and Elizabeth, daughter of a plantation owner and an accomplished artist, created elaborate floral arrangements from the blooming forsythia, dogwoods, and abundance of flowers — including the one that gave Rosedale its name. They spent long afternoons and evenings on the sandbars of the great river, enjoying bonfires with friends and family and living life in a town whose fortunes rose and fell with the level of the river.

The land, the river, and the small town collaborated to make Susanne and Elizabeth the women they are today.

The road out of Rosedale took Susanne Young Reed first to the University of Mississippi in Oxford, where she refined the art of being a Delta girl with sorority life, tailgating in The Grove, and cheering the Ole Miss football team in victory and defeat. Her distinguished academic career at Ole Miss led to a Ph.D. in Education, where she fell in love with what is still referred to in the Deep South as a Yankee. Charlie Reed's profession in forestry management took the couple to south-central Pennsylvania, where they now live with their son, Carter. Susanne enjoys her work as an administrator for Manito, Inc. and as a freelance writer. When life in the rural flatlands of Mississippi meets life in the mountains of rural Pennsylvania, a hilarious clash of cultures ensues, forming the backbone of the stories in this book.

Elizabeth Gourlay Heiskell took another road, one that led back to the Delta and the town of Cleveland, only 20 miles from her family's land in Rosedale. After school at Memphis State University, she married Luke Heiskell, the Delta boy she dreamed of, and they are the parents of three girls, Stott, Mary Paxton, and Lucia. She combined her love of cooking, flower arranging, and entertaining to pursue a culinary life as an accomplished regional caterer and much-loved cooking instructor at the Viking Cooking School, owned by Viking Range Corporation and headquartered in nearby Greenwood, Mississippi. She has cooked for the famous and not-so-famous. She's been a featured teaching chef on Silver Sea Cruises and on television shows such as *The Endless Feast*. Her sense of humor, grace under pressure, flexibility, and immense talent have allowed her to cater memorable events in the most unlikely of places, in fields and tents all over the Deep South. Her recipes and entertaining commentary provide the perfect punctuation for Susanne's stories.

The two little girls from Rosedale grew up to be successful women whose different geographies are united by a rich and colorful past. *Somebody Stole the Cornbread from My Dressing* offers a rare simultaneous peek into two very disparate cultures, and the results are both hilarious and tasty.

Introduction

Welcome to Your
New Culture
(They're Gonna Eat Me Alive)

Each day, on my way to work, I travel over a 2000-foot mountain from the small Pennsylvania town where I now live. I hold my breath until I reach the summit. All the way down the other side, I exhale and think to myself—*fried catfish, football season, hot tamales, cotton, water skis, jug fishing*—and everything else I love about the South.

I am then typically forced back into reality by the loud horns and unkind gestures I receive by the drivers speeding around me. I've been flipped off more times than a pancake at the IHOP. I'm so thankful for car windows, because Lord knows what they are saying as they pass by me with their lips moving to an angry scowl. I just smile and wave, trying to convince them that I truly am a nice person. I often want to follow them to their destination just to tell them we don't have mountains in Mississippi. The tallest thing we have is the levee, and you can't speed on the levee due to all the cows crossing. I don't think they would care. Plus, by the time I've rehearsed what I would say to them ten times, I can only see their taillights in the distance. At that point I am secretly relieved.

When I first moved to this small Northern town, I felt both pure excitement and pure cultural distress. I was in a beautiful new environment—only I was an alien.

"Listen, you'uns, she has an accent," each person would say immediately following introductions. I would just smile, as any Southerner would do, and think to myself, *What is a you'un?* I later discovered that it is their version of y'all. After many encounters such as this one, I began to notice even bigger differences between my Southern and Northern lifestyles.

When they say it is going to snow up here, they are not joking. My first winter here was exciting and frightening all at the same time. I remember waking up and looking out the window that first morning. I nudged my husband (who was not as interested because he has seen a lot of snow in his time) and jumped up to get a better view. It was beautiful, covering the mountains and rooftops. I had never seen such a stunning winter scene.

My happiness quickly turned to fear when I looked out the window onto our driveway. I screamed, "Somebody stole my car!" My husband, a little more interested now, ran to the window. I became enraged as he began to laugh at me. When I questioned his laughter, he just pointed to the tip of an antenna sticking out about three inches above the snow. It was my car antenna. We had gotten so much snow that my car was completely covered. I immediately called my mama, crying, to remind me why I had moved to the North. Then my husband handed me a shovel.

"Ladies don't have to shovel in the South," I quipped.

"Honey, you're in the North now," my husband responded. And again I cried . . . and shoveled . . . and cried.

And they still go to work up here when it snows. Although we had six feet of snow, the roads were cleared in time for morning rush hour (which is not very rushed where I now live). If it just mists snow in Mississippi, everything shuts down completely—except for Walmart, of course.

My husband made it up to me, though. He took me skiing at a local ski resort, a very fancy resort about fifteen minutes from my house. I had heard about this place many times and the wealthy teens who ski there in their free time away from the demanding labors of high school. In their name-brand ski outfits with their name-brand skis and snowboards. I had never been snow skiing before and was very excited to learn. My husband said he would provide me with skiwear. I pictured myself looking so cool, like an L.L.Bean model. That is, until he handed me a pair of Carhartt overalls and hiking boots he'd borrowed from his mother. He wore a matching pair of overalls, and his cousin who joined us had on his matching overalls and work boots. I thought I might die of embarrassment. To this day I blame the overalls for my not being able to snowboard—and for all the snickers I heard each time we got on or off the ski lift.

I've come to love the quirks of this Northern town, just not quite as much as I love Mississippi quirks. I sometimes even miss the Southern-style gossip. Here, they tell you to your face that they don't like your hairstyle or that they think your ideas are stupid (that's never happened to me, of course). I'd much rather they just shared their thoughts about me with someone else in someplace else and leave me out of it—as I've seen it work in the South (not to me, of course).

In reading this book you will learn that deer season is totally different in the North than it is in the South. From baby showers, bridal showers, Thanksgiving, funerals, weddings, and more, this book shares the most exciting adventures I have had while living in the North. I compare them to the Southern versions of my experiences.

Chef Elizabeth Heiskell provides magnificent Southern recipes to complement all aspects of the events featured. We believe that laughter and great food flatter each other extremely well. Our goal is to blend those two items so that you can enjoy a marvelous time with your friends and family.

Through this book Chef Heiskell will teach even the most novice cooks how to deliver fantastic menus at the most important events that can take place throughout your year. She reaches her goal in this book by making cooking enjoyable, easy, and delicious. And she does so with Southern wit and by sharing some of her own hilarious memories regarding her recipes.

Weddings

Curry Dip for Crudités
Crazy Cousin Cheese Bites
Slap Your Sister-in-Law Spicy Pecans
Big Diamond "BLT"
Chandelier Swingin' Artichoke and Crab Dip
Can't Fit Into My Dress Coke and Brown Sugar Ham
Grandmother's Borrowed Biscuits
Make Believe Mayonnaise
Jezebel Sauce
Best Man's Beef Tenderloin
His Hot Date's Horseradish Cream Sauce
Marinated Shrimp
Parmesan Crab Cheese Puffs
Missing Bride's Mojitos

Chapter One
THE USHER'S WIFE

Southern Wedding, n.: A social event where a marriage ceremony is performed (after a few mini-disasters, high drama, and some valium).

When I first moved to the North, I was thrilled to be invited to a wedding. Well, actually my husband was an usher in the wedding and I got to tag along. I didn't know it before, but ushers get a lot of privileges up here. Ushers' wives are not so lucky. After the very lovely wedding, my husband was asked to ride in the limo from the church to the Legion, where the reception was held, with the bride and groom. I drove myself. Once at the Legion, my husband was asked to sit at the table with the wedding party. I sat alone. Then my husband was asked to go through the buffet line (yes, I said buffet line, sneeze guard and all) with the wedding party before anyone else was allowed to eat. I ate my sliced ham, corn, and mashed potatoes with gravy last—and alone.

I was given a "one free drink from the bar" coupon. After spending that coupon—and a few others I "found" because I needed to—I left the party silently screaming, *I gotta go call my mama* in my strongest Southern twang.

Now there was nothing wrong with this Northern wedding. In fact, the wedding itself was gorgeous. It was the reception that was so totally different from what I had experienced in the South. And even though it was different from any of my experiences, it was still a great day.

I've been a bridesmaid five times in Southern weddings. Those experiences gave me vast insight into every single detail of how a wedding is planned and implemented. I say *implemented* because it is with a businesslike intensity that you have to organize and prepare for a Southern wedding. That is probably why I had only eight people at my own wedding, including the pastor and his family, my parents, and my in-laws. But even with a small wedding, there are Southern guidelines to be strictly followed with all aspects of a wedding—from the altar to the bar. (Those are in no particular order, by the way.)

A Southern wedding encompasses every part of elegance—the kind of elegance a Northerner may classify as absurd, but would still be interested in attending. From the sculpted ice in mid-July to live bands, a Southern wedding can be spectacular. Yes, there are plenty of scandalous moves a bride can make in the South, but you will not read about them in the wedding section of the Sunday newspaper, and the perfectly posed pictures will never reflect an ounce of tension. Those slipups are only whispered about in privacy and, of course, without the bride's knowledge.

Chandeliers hanging inside air-conditioned pop-up tents, imported gourmet foods, open bars with the finest options, multilayered cakes, and really expensive flowers that provide aromas for a week after the event. You'll see it all at a Southern wedding. And most of it can be seen resting atop a silver platter—including the wedding planner's reputation, should something go horribly wrong. I used to think all of the outside beauty was used to cover up the inside drama. The bride fighting with her mama over why the wedding dress is fitting a little too tight, or not being able to find the groom who overslept due to a hangover from the bachelor party. Each dollar spent brings a new and juicier dilemma.

No matter what the drama, the end result is always the same—two people married and happy, on an expensive honeymoon, and working on the most fabulous children one could imagine. At least that is what the parents of the couple tell us every single time we run into them at the local Piggly Wiggly.

One thing I've noticed about both Northern and Southern cultures: weddings bring out the best and worst in people, changing the demeanor of those who are involved with the event. Those ordinarily considered party poopers find themselves first on the dance floor, break-dancing to a 1980s classic. And those who normally like to dance on tables at the bar can be quite reserved at the wedding. Weddings can make even those crazy cousins (the ones everybody has) seem a little more tolerable—even when they show up wearing rust-colored outfits with blue flip-flops and spend most of the night talking to the expensive flower arrangements and eating all the snacks at the bar. That is the magic of a Southern wedding.

I guess I am trying to say that although weddings are different—much different—in the North and South, they are both wonderful in their own ways. The most important factors are always apparent: food, drinks, music, family, friends, laughter, and at least one crazy cousin.

Curry Dip for Crudités

It is really important to think outside the box when selecting your vegetables. If I see one more head of raw cauliflower on a crudités tray, I might scream!

1 cup Hellmann's Mayonnaise
3 tablespoons catsup
1 tablespoon Worcestershire sauce
2 tablespoons grated onion
1 tablespoon curry powder
salt to taste
½ teaspoon Tabasco

Mix all ingredients well and chill.

Serve with blanched asparagus, grape tomatoes, cucumbers, blanched green beans, baby carrots, artichoke hearts, radishes with stems, and red, yellow, and orange bell pepper strips. Also serve with cooked, cooled, and quartered new potatoes and zucchini rounds.

In the Delta we love to be fancy by throwing a little of the French language into our sentences. "Crudités" is a prime example—it's just fancy-pants French for raw vegetables.

Crazy Cousin Cheese Bites

Bars at Southern weddings are always adorned with a little nibble. These cheese bites are by far the most popular. We serve them in silver mint julep cups.

2 cups sharp cheddar cheese, shredded
2 cups crisped rice cereal
2 sticks margarine
2 cups flour

⅛ teaspoon garlic powder
½ teaspoon salt
¼ teaspoon red pepper

Preheat oven to 350 degrees. Mix all ingredients well. Roll dough into 2-inch balls and press them with a fork. Bake for 20 minutes.

Normally I would never suggest using margarine. However, in this recipe, butter can make the cheese bites taste greasy. If you are a stickler for butter, feel free to substitute it for the margarine.

Slap Your Sister-in-Law Spicy Pecans

These are great for weddings and just to have on hand in case an unexpected guest arrives at your house for a visit.

1 egg white
1 pound salted and roasted pecans
2 teaspoons cumin
1½ teaspoons cayenne pepper

1 tablespoon water
⅓ cup sugar
2 teaspoons coarse (kosher) salt

Preheat oven to 250 degrees. In a medium bowl, whisk the egg white with 1 tablespoon water until foamy. Add the pecans and toss to coat. Transfer the nuts to a strainer and let drain for at least 2 minutes. In a bowl, combine sugar, cumin, salt, and cayenne pepper. Add the nuts and toss thoroughly to coat. On a large baking sheet with sides, spread the nuts in a single layer. Bake for 40 minutes. Stir with spatula and spread again. Reduce temperature to 200 degrees and bake for 30 minutes more. Using a spatula, loosen the nuts from the baking sheet and let cool on sheet. Do not store before nuts have completely cooled and crisped. They will keep up to a week in an airtight container. Freeze up to 3 months.

Big Diamond BLT

Perfection on white bread!

30 rounds cut from white sandwich bread
3 tablespoons chopped basil
6 small tomatoes, sliced and drained on paper towels
      (when tomatoes are not in season, use Roma or Campari)

1 cup Make Believe Mayonnaise (page 24)
7 strips of cooked bacon, chopped

Cut rounds from bread with a biscuit cutter. Combine mayonnaise and chopped basil. Spread on bread rounds. Top with tomato, sprinkle bacon on top, and serve.

Chandelier Swingin' Artichoke & Crab Dip

Silver chafing dishes are a must for a Southern wedding. They always contain something creamy and wonderful. This dip is no exception.

6 cans artichoke hearts, drained and quartered
1 8-ounce package cream cheese, room temperature
1 pound of fresh crabmeat

½ cup Hellmann's Mayonnaise
½ cup Parmesan cheese
Pastry shells (page 105)

Drain artichoke hearts and process in a food processor until finely chopped. Add mayonnaise, cream cheese, and Parmesan cheese. Fold crabmeat in gently. Bake at 350 degrees for 30 minutes. Serve in a chafing dish with pastry shells.

Never, ever, under any circumstances put any type of chip on your dining room table. We recommend Carr's Table Water Crackers, toast points, or pastry shells.

Can't Fit Into My Dress
Coke & Brown Sugar Ham

Coca-Cola and pork. Need I say more? Could it get any better? Yes, when served with Grandmother's Borrowed Biscuits!

14-16-pound spiral cut ham
2 cups brown sugar
3 tablespoons orange zest

1 12-ounce can of Coke
½ cup spicy brown mustard
¼ cup orange juice

Mix glaze ingredients. Pour into medium sauce pan and warm on medium-low to medium heat until sugar melts. Place ham on a foil-lined, rimmed baking sheet. Coat ham with mixture. Place in oven at 350 degrees. Baste every 30 minutes and bake according to package directions.

Grandmother's Borrowed Biscuits

These dainty biscuits are a Southern staple. Use a small biscuit cutter. There is nothing more vulgar than a biscuit the size of someone's fist!

2 cups flour, sifted
½ teaspoon salt
4 teaspoons baking powder (rounded)
⅔ cup milk

2 teaspoons sugar
½ teaspoon cream of tartar
½ cup shortening

Mix dry ingredients together. Cut in shortening until it resembles coarse corn meal. Add the milk in thirds and mix lightly. Form dough into a ball and place on a floured board. Pat dough into a 2-inch-thick disk and use a 3-inch cookie cutter to cut rounds. At this point the biscuits can be frozen or are ready to bake. Place in oven at 450 degrees and bake until lightly brown, approximately 12-15 minutes.

When mixing shortening into ingredients, use your fingers.
Sometimes fingers can be the best cooking utensil.

Make-Believe Mayonnaise

I believe in homemade mayonnaise, but I am also a realist. Few people have the time to make homemade mayonnaise—especially for 300 hungry wedding guests.

2 cups Hellmann's Mayonnaise

1 tablespoon Tony Chachere's Creole Seasoning

juice of one lemon

Mix ingredients. Can be kept in your refrigerator for up to two weeks.

A note about Hellmann's Mayonnaise . . . there is no better brand!
I have almost come to blows about the importance of using Hellmann's over other brands of mayonnaise.

Jezebel Sauce

I'm not sure why this is called Jezebel Sauce, except it's easy and has been passed around more than an offering plate. It's been whispered about for decades and is always a hit with the boys!

1 cup apple jelly

¼ cup French's Mustard

1 cup orange marmalade

½ cup prepared horseradish sauce

Mix all ingredients and serve with pork, ham, chicken, or shrimp.

Best Man's Beef Tenderloin

This is always the most popular item on the menu. Regardless of how many times it is served, we never grow tired of it. This dish can distinguish a wedding and give the guests something to talk about the next day.

1 5-6 pound cooked beef tenderloin, room temperature
1 tablespoon Worcestershire sauce
salt and pepper

1 stick of butter, softened
2 cloves garlic, minced

Preheat oven to 500 degrees. Pat tenderloin dry with a paper towel. Mix the butter, Worcestershire sauce, and garlic. Generously coat the tenderloin with mixture. Salt and pepper liberally. Place tenderloin on a rimmed baking sheet that has been covered with foil. Roast for 25 minutes for rare and 28 minutes for medium rare. Remove from oven and cover with foil. Allow tenderloin to rest for at least 10 to 15 minutes. The filet will continue to cook. Slice thin and mound on silver trays. Serve with Parker House rolls and Horseradish Cream Sauce (recipe below).

Overseasoning pre-cooked meat with salt and pepper is very difficult. Be generous with those ingredients. Seasoning meat once it has been cooked is quite hard, so go for it on the front end.

His Hot Date's Horseradish Cream Sauce

1 cup sour cream
6 tablespoons prepared horseradish
1 teaspoon salt

½ cup Hellmann's Mayonnaise
1 teaspoon pepper

Combine well and refrigerate until ready to use.

Marinated Shrimp

Because shrimp can be expensive depending on where you live and the season, vegetables not only add color, but they also help give you more bang for your buck.

5 pounds of 21/25 count shrimp
dressing (see recipe below)
2 cans artichoke hearts, drained and quartered

3 tablespoons Zatarain's Liquid Crab Boil
2 boxes grape tomatoes

Peel and devein shrimp. Bring a large pot of water to a boil. Add Zatarain's Liquid Crab Boil and shrimp. Cook for 3-4 minutes. Drain and pour ice on top to stop the cooking process. Once cooled, drain very well. Combine with dressing. Add grape tomatoes and quartered artichoke hearts. Put in fridge for at least 3-4 hours. Can be served up to 24 hours after preparation.

Dressing

2 tablespoons Hellmann's Mayonnaise
2 large garlic cloves, chopped
2 teaspoons salt
1½ cups mild olive oil

2 teaspoons Dijon mustard
¼ cup freshly squeezed lemon juice
½ teaspoon black pepper

Using a food processor, mix mayonnaise, mustard, garlic, lemon juice, salt, and pepper until smooth. Slowly drizzle olive oil while processor is running. If the mixture becomes too thick, add a tablespoon of water to thin it. If you don't have a processor, simply whisk ingredients until smooth then slowly drizzle olive oil as you continue to whisk.

Drizzling the oil slowly is key to any vinaigrette. Oil and acid are not fond of one another.
The whisk is the marriage counselor between them both.
Adding air between the oil and the acid helps to bond them together.

Parmesan Crab Puffs

1 cup Hellmann's Mayonnaise
½ cup grated Parmesan cheese
½ cup fresh crabmeat
1 loaf sliced white bread

1 teaspoon Tony Chachere's Creole Seasoning
2 teaspoons lemon juice
½ teaspoon Worcestershire sauce

Mix all ingredients except for white bread. Use a biscuit cutter to cut circles in the white bread. Spread mixture on bread rounds. Toast in a 350-degree oven until bubbly, approximately 12-15 minutes.

Missing Bride's Mojitos

A signature drink is a lovely thing to pass on silver trays as guests arrive. A fantastic drink!

sprigs of fresh mint
1 teaspoon sugar
⅛ teaspoon lime juice

crushed ice
2 ounces rum
club soda

Mash mint sprigs in a highball glass and fill with crushed ice. Add the rum, sugar, and lime juice and fill with club soda. Stir. Garnish with fresh mint.

Tailgating

Pimento Cheese Sandwiches
Deloris's Fight Your Best Friend for It Fried Chicken
Avocado Salsa with Blue Corn Chips
Sober Me Up Egg and Olive Sandwiches
Big Will's Bloody Mary
Peanut Butter Bars

Chapter Two
FOUR QUARTERS & A TAILGATE

Southern Tailgating, v.: to participate in a picnic that is served from the tailgate of a vehicle, as before a sporting event. If only it were that simple.

There was a particular day when I actually cried about the differences between my new, small hometown in Pennsylvania and my hometown in Mississippi—when I learned there was no football in my county. I was devastated by this news. My father was a very successful Mississippi football coach, Leland Young. I love the game.

So many questions raced through my head: *What do they do on Friday nights up here? What do they talk about on Saturday mornings? What do they yearn for as each school year begins? Do they have cheerleaders? Lord, why me?*

Then I remembered the next-best thing to Friday night football games: Saturday football games. College football and tailgating—two activities that brighten the entire fall season. I decided to go to a Northern football game—a great idea, so I thought.

I wore my finest dress with matching shoes. I spent an hour on my makeup and hair and had my picnic basket filled with baked goods, cheese, wine, and silverware. I walked to the tailgating area of this Northern university and saw nothing but cars from one end to the other. I was so excited. I entered the grassy area, and that is when it happened. I heard a loud screeching sound—the kind that only I could hear—that halted all music and conversations from entering my ears. It sent a flushed feeling throughout my body and turned my expansive smile into a sort of mangled look of confusion.

Have you ever entered a room and all eyes turned toward you, and everyone stops talking so that they can focus their stares directly at you? The kind of stare that makes you want to check your skirt to make sure it is not caught in your pantyhose, exposing your backside to the world. The kind of stare that makes you get to a mirror with lightning speed to make sure there are no leftovers on your face or in your teeth. Well, that is what happened to me.

I instantly knew what was wrong. As my eyes scanned the crowd, I noticed most people wearing jeans or cutoffs and oversized jerseys endorsing their favorite players, all holding plastic cups filled with a variety of mixtures, all having a great time. They are very literal in the North. To tailgate means to tail gate, and every enthusiastic fan could simply reach into their trunks for refills of food and drink. Car radios blared country music, and face painting was the norm—except when paint could be applied elsewhere on the body. Nothing was really off-limits.

And now with every oversized foam finger pointing to me instead of toward the sky, all I wanted to do was run. And that is exactly what I did. I ran back to my car, changed into comfortable clothing that I had brought along for evening events, and headed back to the game. On the way back, I bought my own foam finger and pointed my way through the crowd. To tell you the truth, the fans I met that day were true champions, true supporters, who were there because they love the game and their team. It was a great time.

I am sure if any one of these Northern football fans went to an SEC tailgating party, they would have lots of stories to tell their family and friends upon return. However, until my Northern experience, I never really thought tailgating in The Grove at Ole Miss was abnormal. Tailgating to me meant lines of white tents surrounding The Grove and encompassing many social meetings and greetings. I remember the fold-out tables were covered in the finest tablecloths. Chandeliers hung from inside their tents with floral arrangements as beautiful centerpieces. Some families even brought their best silver with them. Why should tailgating be different than

any other day? And if you are going to have a few toddies before the game, it is imperative to drink them from the finest glassware. Everything is monogrammed—from the coolers to the napkins to our personalized foam fingers (which we would also point at those who were new to the scene). The atmosphere is extremely traditional in nature, even when it comes to the food brought by the fans.

I remember the friendliness of each family occupying the tents and their willingness to share food, drinks, and even the occasional walk to the Union to use the restrooms. The only thing louder than the cheers and chants on those Saturdays was the smell of hard liquor hovering in the trees. The best liquor was consumed on such occasions and was always supplemented by some homemade concoctions. Even the blades of grass caught a buzz.

Tailgating in the South is one time when the women wear dresses so fine they could leave the football game and attend a cocktail party without having to make a wardrobe change. The women dressed this fine simply to complement their equally clad male counterparts. From neatly coifed hair to ancestors' jewels, both men and women are impressive.

The social element of tailgating was so important. It was here, in The Grove, that you could network with future employers, be set up on a date with the offspring of a prominent community member, be groomed for a sorority or fraternity, and even be swept away in a political debate. Of course, every once in a while, you might notice a debutante who had had a bit too much to drink, looking perfect even as she stumbled from one tent to the next, searching for her own monogrammed seat. And her dear sweet beau, right behind her catching every drop that sloshed out of her mixed drink.

The moment of the day that created the most excitement was the Walk of Champions, when the players made their way through the crowds and to the stadium. Hundreds of tailgaters lined the path, and players did their best to avoid being tackled by adoring fans. If you didn't get goose bumps during this time, you were not a true fan. This moment bridged the gap between player and fan and made us feel like we were actually a part of the team. After the players left, it was back to socializing and eating even more great food — mostly fried.

It was then time to make our way to our seats in the stadium to cheer for the team we love, the Rebels, shouting all the way, "Hotty Toddy, Gosh almighty. Who the hell are we, Hey! Flim flam, bim bam. Ole Miss, by damn!" The Hotty Toddy lyrics are usually the first words spoken by a toddler whose parents are Ole Miss Fans — even before "mama" or "dada."

There are numerous commonalities between Northern and Southern tailgating events. Both sets of fans are loyal to their teams and to the game of football. Both sides love to combine food and drink in a social atmosphere. And both cultures appreciate a good rivalry.

If you are preparing for a tailgating event in either the North or the South, the most important thing to remember is to have fun. And don't forget your foam finger, just in case somebody new arrives on the scene.

Pimento Cheese Sandwiches

Many people call this "Mississippi Pâte." I call it "Heaven."

2 cups white cheddar cheese, shredded (Buy the block and shred it yourself. It makes a huge difference.)
1 cup Hellmann's Mayonnaise, no substitution
½ cup shredded Parmesan cheese
6 ounces roasted red peppers, diced
        (You can find the peppers in the specialty section of your grocery store.)
¼ cup chopped pecans
¼ cup chopped green onions
¼ teaspoon Tabasco
¼ teaspoon Tony Chachere's Creole Seasoning
¼ teaspoon Worcestershire sauce

Mix all ingredients together. Serve as a sandwich or a spread for crackers.

Deloris's Fight Your Best Friend for It Fried Chicken

Making friends is easy when you are tailgating with Deloris's fried chicken. It is delicious when hot, cold, or at room temperature. Perfect for game day!

1 package assorted chicken pieces
2 tablespoons Tony Chachere's Creole Seasoning
1 gallon peanut oil

4 cups all-purpose flour
¼ cup seasoned salt

Mix dry ingredients then taste. You may need to adjust the seasoning to fit your taste. (The first time I was told to taste those ingredients, I liketa died, but it is the only way to ensure it is seasoned correctly. So now I gladly taste the flour every time.) Pour flour mix into a paper bag. Add chicken and shake until well coated. Pour peanut oil into a deep fat fryer. Fry until the chicken is golden and floats on top of the oil. Timing will vary by piece. It is important to wait for the chicken to float to the top of the oil. Drain on a paper bag covered with paper towels.

Avocado Salsa & Blue Corn Chips

Serve with a mix of blue and white corn chips, and people will really think ya did something. Sometimes it is all about the presentation!

2 chopped tomatoes
4 ripe avocados cut into cubes
¼ cup chopped cilantro
½ medium onion, diced
salt and pepper

2 limes, juiced
½ jalapeno pepper, diced, discard seeds
¼ teaspoon cumin
¼ teaspoon chili powder

Mix well. Let sit in refrigerator for at least one hour. Add salt and pepper to taste. Press plastic wrap on the top of the salsa to prevent oxidation of the avocados, or put it in a freezer bag and make sure to remove all the air.

Sober Me Up Egg & Olive Sandwiches

My husband's family wouldn't dream of going to The Grove without this sandwich. There are some absolutes in life: death, taxes, and that on game day, Luke Heiskell will be in The Grove with Egg & Olive Sandwiches and a good Bloody Mary (see page 39 for recipe).

1 dozen hard-boiled eggs, chopped
½ jar (12 oz.) olives with pimentos
½ cup Hellmann's Mayonnaise
   (don't you dare substitute anything else)

¼ cup cooked, chopped bacon
salt and pepper, generously
¼ teaspoon Tabasco

Mix ingredients, spread on wheat or white bread.

For a variation, cut the crust off bread and cut sandwiches into diagonal slices.
Stand on the cut side to make a nice presentation, because although good, white bread ain't too pretty.
Let the filling do the talking.

Big Will's Bloody Mary

All Southern girls think their daddies makes the best Bloody Mary. I am no exception. When we were growing up, as soon as Daddy left the Baptist church on Sunday morning, he would head straight for the kitchen to make up this wonderful concoction.

1 48-ounce bottle V8 juice
¾ cup fresh lime juice
4 tablespoons prepared horseradish
3 tablespoons Worcestershire sauce
1 teaspoon salt
½ teaspoon pepper
1½ cups vodka
1 teaspoon celery salt

Blend all but the vodka and celery salt. Mix vodka in right before serving. Store up to one week.

Run a lime around the rim of the glass and pour celery salt on a plate. Invert the glass to celery salt the rim. Don't forget pickled okra and a green bean for extra garnish. The glass will look like a salad once you have the celery stalk, green bean, lime, and okra, but it will offset all the vodka. You gotta get your veggies somehow!

Peanut Butter Bars

If Deloris's Fried Chicken will help make a friend, this recipe will make best friends.

1 cup butter
1 cup peanut butter
1 1-pound package powdered sugar
1½ cups crushed vanilla wafers
½ cup heavy whipping cream
1 12-ounce package chocolate chips

In a stand mixer fitted with a paddle attachment, combine butter, peanut butter, and powdered sugar until well mixed. Add vanilla wafers, mix until blended well, and press mixture into a 9x13 casserole dish. Put in refrigerator to chill. In the meantime, warm heavy cream in a medium saucepan. Remove from heat and add chocolate chips and stir until melted. Pour over peanut butter mixture. Place in refrigerator to stiffen. Cut into squares.

If you are like Susanne and do not have a stand mixer or a clue what the heck a paddle attachment is, just make sure the butter is at room temperature and very soft. By hand, combine the butter, peanut butter, and powdered sugar.

New Year's Eve

Fried Pork Chops
Bring on the Luck Black-Eyed Pea Salad
Midnight Kiss Mustard Greens with Ham Hocks
Toast Worthy Fried Green Tomatoes
Consommé Rice
Call Me Next Year Come Back Sauce
Bird's Dream Big Cornbread
Henry's Green Sauce
Grandmother's Buttermilk Cake
Bye-Bye Resolutions Banana Pudding

Chapter Three
SHOTGUNS, BEER, & A HAPPY NEW YEAR

Southern New Year's Eve Party, n.: An event that takes place on January 31st, usually a formal occasion giving people an excuse to dress up, drink, dance, and dream big. That's before midnight.

New Year's Eve is a time of celebration, laughter, and hope. Whether in the North or the South, people are filled with a renewed spirit and optimism about the upcoming year. Wide-ranging visions include lonely people finding a soul mate, jobless finding work, babies being conceived and born, promotions, soldiers returning home from war, and more. The more simplistic dreams include weight loss, healthier living, and finally breaking a few bad habits. While there are universal wishes and traditions that span the globe, there are also more localized traditions that are quite different depending on where you live.

The first New Year's Eve I spent in the North was very educational. I learned how to make cracklins in a large black kettle and that when bullets are shot up into the clear night sky, they don't always come straight back down. I also learned about homemade potato guns, which, as it turns out, are very dangerous weapons. The best thing I learned is that you don't have to be formally dressed to have a great party, unlike a lot of the parties I have attended in the South.

The party we attended was in a huge metal storage building sitting next to the host's house. We had great food, great drinks, and great company. And if you mix those three things with fried fat, you have the beginning of a great New Year's Eve experience. Everyone was dressed in Levi's jeans, boots, and comfortable outerwear to keep them warm on the cold night.

After a couple of hours of celebrating, one of the guests brought out the homemade potato gun. This concoction could shoot a potato across the room at a speed so fast it put a dent in the side of the metal building. And when he asked, "Hey, do you guys think a potato gun could kill someone?" I knew we were in for an interesting night.

Midnight drew closer and closer, and I noticed all the guys at the party heading outside. I stayed inside with the women, even though I was extremely curious about what the men might be up to. Then the countdown began, "Five, four, three, two, one."

BANG BANG BANG BANG BANG BANG BANG BANG BANG! Gunshots roared through the night air, I hit the floor screaming, and a potato shot through a few trees, breaking several limbs along the way.

Living close to Gettysburg, you can imagine my first thought: General Robert E. Lee had rerouted his ghostly soldiers in the direction of our New Year's Eve party. It truly sounded like the Civil War outside that storage building. The women laughed, of course, and led me outside to where the men were all reloading their weapons for another round. Apparently it is a tradition for my husband and his friends to shoot their firearms at midnight on New Year's Eve to ring in the New Year.

"Where are the fireworks?" I asked.

"They're illegal in Pennsylvania," they all responded in unison.

"And shooting bullets and potatoes while drinking is legal?" I continued.

"Yes," they responded.

I was terrified, but what is a nice Southern girl supposed to do in a situation like this? So I grabbed the gun from my husband and began to fire it straight up in the sky with my eyes shut completely tight. I finished firing, opened my eyes, and noticed everyone around me was on the ground. No, they weren't laughing. They were in fear for their lives, scared to death I was going to accidentally kill them. Even though I grew up around guns, it was quite obvious I was not comfortable using one. That discomfort carried over to everyone else at the party that night, especially when I asked, "Can I try the potato gun now?"

After reassuring everyone that I was not crazy, that I was just trying to fit in, my husband informed me it was time to go home. Everyone laughed it off, but I am sure they are still talking about me today and how their lives were in danger because of a crazy Southern woman. I have to say, ringing in the New Year with a rifle was a lot of fun. And although I've never been allowed to do that again, that night will always have a special place in my heart.

My husband was not as thrilled. He lectured me the whole way home about the dangers of guns and safety precautions I should take when shooting a firearm. He even made me take the hunter's safety course with a bunch of 12-year-old little boys later that year.

The next day, New Year's Day, we went to a family member's house for the traditional New Year's good luck meal. I was so ready for some black-eyed peas. For over 30 years of living in the South, I started each New Year with a heaping helping of black-eyed peas, placing all my dreams for the year in each bite. One spoonful of black-eyed peas meant that I would finally lose that extra 20 pounds I needed to lose. Okay, 30 pounds. And additional spoonfuls meant that I would find a more satisfying job, have a more positive attitude, gossip less, build a better relationship with God, and of course, start exercising.

After that many spoonfuls of black-eyed peas, I was so full I'd have to lie down, take a nap, pray that God would help me get over the sick feeling, and talk negatively to myself because I was now too tired to search for a new job or exercise. Since I had already broken all the other resolutions, I then would call a friend to catch up on the latest gossip. I would end the day with a few more black-eyed peas for good measure and tell myself repeatedly, *Tomorrow is a new day. You will start again in the morning and you will be successful at reaching your resolutions this year. And if you don't start tomorrow, then you can start next Monday. And if you can't start on Monday, wait until the first day of the next month. And if you can't start then, wait until summer when it is warmer and you can get outside to walk. Don't worry; you have 364 days to prove you can do it.* (Self-talk and affirmation have never really been strengths of mine.)

I couldn't wait to do the same now that I was living in the North with my new husband. I thought there was no way I could fail at my resolutions now since my life had already changed so much. Boy was I naïve.

As soon as we walked into the house, I could smell something. And it was *not* black-eyed peas. I asked my husband, "What's that smell?"

"Sauerkraut," he joyfully responded. "And pork and shrimp. That's what we have every New Year's Day for good luck."

I thought to myself, *I'm just going to eat the black-eyed peas and mashed potatoes (because I knew there would be mashed potatoes) and that would be enough.* We said grace, thanked God for family and food, and began passing the feast. I waited and watched. First around the table was a baked corn casserole. Delicious. Next was the sauerkraut. Passed. Next was the pork. Passed. Then the shrimp. Delicious, but could have been a bit more Cajun. And then the mashed potatoes that were delicious, as usual. And that was it. I waited and waited and waited but saw no black-eyed peas. I turned my head all the way around (think *The Exorcist*) to see if maybe they were still cooking on the stove in the kitchen—but no pots were there. My eyes scanned the countertops for even a can of black-eyed peas. Nothing. My husband finally asked, "What are you looking for?"

"Nothing," I responded, embarrassed that I was not as sly as I thought.

"What is it?" the host chimed in. "Are we missing anything?"

"Well, are there any black-eyed peas?" I asked.

"Black-eyed peas?" She chuckled.

"I just need a spoonful or two," I said. "I don't have that many resolutions this year."

"No, we don't have any black-eyed peas. We have sweet peas, though. Want some of those?" she politely offered.

"No, thanks." I was devastated. Well, not really, but still disappointed. I wondered how sauerkraut and pork could bring better luck than black-eyed peas? And what does shrimp have to do with anything? I continued my silent pity party all the way through two helpings of the baked corn casserole and mashed potatoes, and even through some apple dumplings. I was feeling a bit drowsy, as most do when they over-stuff themselves, so I waddled to the couch and thought, *Not having black-eyed peas has already made me break one of my resolutions, to diet. Because there were no black-eyed peas, I just had to eat all those mashed potatoes. Now I don't even feel like exercising because I'm so full of that fattening food.* Continuing to take no responsibility for overeating and feeling like crap, I took a nap and dreamed about New Year's in the South.

The New Year's Eve parties I've been to in the South are quite different from the ones in the North. There aren't any potato guns, there are no real live firearms, and no ammunition at all unless you count the alcohol. No one is dressed for comfort, only for style. Women are limping because their feet hurt from the Jimmy Choo shoes they are wearing. But hey, they are Jimmy Choos, even if they are a size too small. That's how women in the South buy shoes—for name brand and style, not comfort. If a woman wears a size 7 in the South, you will be able to look in her closet and find a range of sizes from 6 to 8, all designer. If the store didn't have her size, but she really wanted the name-brand shoes, she will make her foot fit into those shoes no matter what.

Same goes for her clothing. If a Southern woman is a size 10 but wants to be a size 8 on New Year's Eve, there is a girdle out there to help her fit into whatever clothing she desires. There are the leg shapers, the back smoothers, the butt lifters, the boob minimizers, the hip huggers, the belly busters, the curve correctors, and the full-bodied jumpsuit girdle that erases all bumps and rolls from the nape of the neck to the ankles. There are even T-shirt girdles to reduce the size of a woman's arms from wildly stout to slightly oversized. All for the sake of beauty, women in the South will go to extremes to make themselves perfect for a night on the town. And believe you me, it is all worth it when that handsome beau escorts his lovely date through the party's entrance, and all the other women stop what they are doing to "recognize" you. If you get the full look, eyes shifting from shoes to hair, then you have done something right. The full look means other women are jealous and will probably talk about you to their friends while primping in the ladies' room.

The women aren't the only things looking their best at a New Year's Eve party. The food looks like it jumped from the pages of *Southern Living*, and the home of the host looks just as flawless. There is usually a fully stocked bar, with drinks being served out of crystal, and napkins monogrammed with the host's initials. A catered buffet of food will be the centerpiece of the house that night. The food will be fancy and fabulous; some items will be hard to pronounce but easy to eat. However, there is nothing in the buffet that is too heavy or that will interfere with the feeling the spirits from the bar can offer. And with a constant stream of people moving throughout the home, the host knows she has once again thrown a party that will be talked about for at least the first week of January.

The countdown at a Southern New Year's Eve party is much more reserved—everyone wanting to yell loudly but not wanting to embarrass themselves or solidify their place as the person being gossiped about that next week. So they hold up their engraved glasses, toast, and laugh their way into a great new year.

Not all Southern parties are so formal. In fact, there are plenty of Southern parties that involve only cheap beer and a box of firecrackers. However, nothing beats a good ole formal, traditional New Year's where for one night you act classier, eat fancier, drink more tastefully, and dream bigger than you have the entire year before.

Both Northern and Southern parties are great times with a lot of great people. Southerners could certainly learn a few things from Northerners about how to have a good time, and vice versa. I'd love to see my dear Northern friends wear formal attire to one of their parties—or at least have a cup or napkin monogrammed. And I'd love to see a few potato guns and cracklins at a traditional Southern party. And for just one year, I'd like to eat my black-eyed peas and reach every single goal I set. But then again, I'd hate to mess with tradition.

These are all very good recipes with the perfect amount of grease to help recover from the liquor fever you caught while ringing in the New Year. If you think cooking through tears for a funeral is tough, cooking while hung over is ten times worse. These recipes are simple, simple, simple.

Fried Pork Chops

6 bone-in pork chops, no more than one-inch thick, rinsed and patted dry
3 cups flour
2 tablespoons seasoned salt
1 tablespoon Tony Chachere's Creole Seasoning
salt and pepper to taste
5 cups peanut oil

Fill a medium-sized black iron skillet with tall sides with the oil and bring to 300 degrees, using a thermometer to judge the temperature. Meanwhile, place the flour and seasonings in a shallow dish and mix well. Taste the flour to make sure it has enough seasoning. It should be a little over-seasoned in order for the meat to have the correct flavor. Dredge each pork chop through the flour and place in the oil. Fry until golden brown and an instant-read meat thermometer registers 140 degrees on the interior, about 6–10 minutes.

Peanut oil has the highest smoke point and should always be used for frying, because it can reach high temperatures without burning.

Bring on the Luck Black-Eyed Pea Salad

In the South, black-eyed peas are eaten on New Year's Day for good luck in the coming year. I always eat three or four portions for good measure!

4 15-ounce cans black-eyed peas, drained
7 slices of bacon, cooked and chopped
2 tablespoons bacon grease
1 can artichoke hearts, drained, quartered, and roughly chopped
½ red pepper, diced
1 jar pepper sauce (I prefer Braswell's Pepper Relish)
salt and pepper to taste

Mix all ingredients and let sit overnight in refrigerator. Serve at room temperature.

In the summer, roasted fresh corn is a great addition to this salad.

Midnight Kiss Mustard Greens with Ham Hocks

Deloris taught me everything there is to know about greens—a gift that keeps on giving. I don't think any other green comes close to mustard greens. If you wish, you can substitute turnip or collard greens. I wouldn't, but you will still get good results.

4 bunches of mustard greens, cleaned well
1 medium smoked ham hock
1 fresh chili pepper or 2 teaspoons dried chili flakes
1 tablespoon seasoned salt
1 tablespoon Tony Chachere's Creole Seasoning
2 tablespoons canola oil

Fill a large pot with water and add ham hock, chili pepper or flakes, salt, Creole Seasoning, and oil. Bring to a boil and then cut down to a simmer for at least 30 minutes. The spices must permeate the water so the greens will take on that flavor. After tasting the water to make sure it has enough flavor, add the greens. Simmer for one hour until very tender.

Toast Worthy Fried Green Tomatoes

3 green tomatoes
2 teaspoons seasoned salt
1 tablespoon Tony Chachere's Creole Seasoning
salt and pepper to taste

1 cup buttermilk
3 cups flour
peanut oil for frying

Slice the tomatoes ½ inch thick. Toss with buttermilk and let sit while oil is heating to 350 degrees. Mix flour and seasonings in a shallow pan. Take 1 slice of tomato, shake off excess buttermilk, then dredge in flour and shake off excess again. Place in the hot oil and fry until golden brown. Serve with Come Back Sauce (next page).

For a lovely first course, add shrimp or lump crab meat on top.

Call Me Next Year Come Back Sauce

This sauce originated at Mayflower Cafe in Jackson, Mississippi. Everyone kept "coming back" for this wonderful sauce, except my cousin who behaved badly having had a little too much wine at the restaurant. He was asked never to come back.

¼ cup onion, grated on the large side of a box grater
¼ cup chili sauce
1 tablespoon Worcestershire sauce
1 teaspoon salt

½ cup vegetable oil
3 tablespoons lemon juice
1 teaspoon dry mustard
1 teaspoon pepper

Mix all ingredients together. If sauce is too thick to drizzle, add 1 tablespoon of water to thin. This is also wonderful as a dip for crudités, boiled shrimp, fried crab claws . . . hell — everything goes with this delicious sauce.

Consommé Rice

This recipe was one of my mother's go-to luncheon items at the Rotary Club Luncheon in Rosedale, Mississippi. People came out of the woodwork on the day it was Momma and Ms. Searcy's turn to provide lunch.

¼ cup butter
1 cup uncooked rice
2 tablespoons soy sauce

1 cup onions, finely chopped
2 cans consommé

Preheat oven to 350 degrees. Melt butter in a skillet and add onions. Cook until lightly browned. Add the rice until also lightly browned, but not burned, and then add the consommé and soy sauce. Place the entire mixture into a casserole dish and bake for an hour.

Bird's Dream Big Cornbread

In the South we have an uncanny ability to nickname people even when they are just toddlers. When Tara's grandmother said she acts "just like a bird," no truer words have ever been spoken. This is Bird's recipe that breaks my low-carb diet every single time. It's almost light as a cake and just as wonderful. Many from the South would say sugar in cornbread is sacrilegious. Some even go so far as to say it was one of the reasons the Civil War was fought. Right or wrong—I promise you will love this recipe.

2 cups self-rising flour
2 cups white self-rising cornmeal
¼ cup sugar
2 eggs
½ cup buttermilk
12 tablespoons oil

Mix flour, cornmeal, and sugar in one bowl. In another bowl whisk eggs with buttermilk and add dry ingredients. The mixture should be as thick as cake batter. Add more buttermilk if it is too dry, more cornmeal if it is too thin. Pour oil evenly into muffin pan (1 tablespoon per muffin cup). Heat muffin pan in 400-degree oven for 5-7 minutes. Carefully pour the hot oil into the cornbread mixture. Stir well. Pour batter into the muffin cups and cook until golden brown, about 25 minutes.

Henry's Green Sauce

2½ cups olive oil
6 cloves garlic, finely chopped
2 bunches parsley, chopped
¼ cup balsamic vinegar
¼ cup red wine vinegar
4 teaspoons Dijon mustard
2 tablespoons lemon juice
1 3½-ounce jar of capers
3 teaspoons anchovy paste
½ cup fresh mint
1 teaspoon salt

Blend together all ingredients and serve with lamb, beef, pork, chicken, or shrimp. Hell, you can put it with anything. It couldn't be more versatile, and once you try it, you will see why John felt the need to burgle his neighbor for the recipe. See the story below!

Many Southerners are reluctant to give out their prized family recipes. I guess they feel that being able to make something better than anyone else makes them more special, and if everyone can make the dish, then maybe they won't shine as bright. The story of Henry's Green Sauce is one of these circumstances, and this is how it was told to me. Evelyn and John were two longtime friends who loved to cook and entertain. Evelyn had been to John's house and fell in love with his apple tart. John was happy to give the recipe to her. However, Evelyn would not return the favor when John asked for her caper sauce recipe. At that point, John decided he would get that recipe no matter what it took. Not too long after, Evelyn went out of town for the weekend. John asked Henry—a handyman they both used—if he had the keys to Evelyn's house, because John had loaned her a book and wanted to get it back right away. Henry gave John the keys, and John found the recipe box and proceeded to copy the caper sauce recipe as well as a few others he was fond of. Once Evelyn returned to town, John invited her over for dinner and served lamb with the caper sauce. He told Evelyn, "I have been trying to duplicate your sauce. Please tell me what you think." Evelyn tasted it, waited, and spoke one word: "Almost."

Grandmother's Buttermilk Cake

This recipe has become my grandmother's calling card when she visits her grandchildren. God forbid she ever try to come through our doors without it.

3 cups sugar
¼ teaspoon salt
3 cups cake flour
1 teaspoon vanilla or almond extract

1 cup shortening
6 eggs
1 cup buttermilk, divided into ¾ cup and ¼ cup
¼ teaspoon baking soda

In a stand mixer, blend the sugar, shortening, and salt until creamy. Slowly add each egg until all six are beaten into the mixture. Sift the cake flour three times then add to the mixture. Add ¾ cup buttermilk and the vanilla or almond extract. Add ¼ cup buttermilk with the baking soda and fold with a spoon 150 strokes. Pour into a greased and floured angel food tube pan. Place into a cold oven. Bake at 300 degrees for 1½ hours. During the last ten minutes, turn off the oven. Turn out of the pan while still hot.

Bye-Bye Resolutions Banana Pudding

Most banana pudding recipes use custard as the base. My co-worker at Viking Cooking School, Becky, would just die if she knew this recipe was going into print. She loves custard and thinks there is no other way to make banana pudding. Maybe she is right, but sometimes we get tired and need an easy way out! This recipe is easy, good, and quick.

2 3-ounce packages vanilla or banana instant pudding
8 ounces sour cream
8 ounces Cool Whip, thawed
4 bananas, peeled and sliced

2 cups milk
14 ounces sweetened condensed milk
12 ounces vanilla wafers

Mix the instant pudding, milk, sour cream, condensed milk, and Cool Whip well. In a 3-quart dish alternate layers of the pudding mixture, bananas, and wafers, ending with vanilla wafers on the top. Chill in the refrigerator for 2–3 hours.

Susan, thank you for the use of this recipe!

Funerals

Sometimes breakfast items are overlooked, but they can be a welcome change from the 32 hams the grieving family has already received.

Four Cheese Garlic Grits
Delivered by Angels Asparagus and Egg Casserole
Sausage Pinwheels
Better than Counseling Curried Fruit

Something to Gossip About Pork Tenderloin
Orange Soy Sauce
Comfort Your Soul Chicken, Artichoke, & Wild Rice Casserole
Marinated Vegetables
Coconut Glop Cake
Chocolate Chip Bundt Cake

Chapter Four
SOMEBODY DIED . . .
SO WHERE'S THE FOOD?

Southern Funeral Food, n.: elaborate food dishes either bought or baked with the intent of comforting the grieving family . . . and being good enough to make it through the gossip rounds the following week.

I don't know what it is, but there is just something about hearing of a death that sends a Southern woman straight to the kitchen. Her eyes begin to glisten, her heart paces, and she loses just a touch of focus as she scatters through her kitchen for ingredients. She ties on her monogrammed apron and creates some good ole homemade comfort food that will enable the mourners to temporarily escape their grief. That doesn't happen, of course, but it does help all of those visiting the family feel better and offers the chef more than a few compliments.

In the South, before the word can spread from one end of town to the next, women set their stoves and ovens at the appropriate temperature to create the most kindly dishes possible. You will see more variety of food at a grieving family's house than you do at a Ryan's buffet on a Saturday night. Macaroni and cheese in at least four different varieties, fried chicken, chocolate cake, lemon squares, and every form of casserole handed down from generation to generation. It's almost as if the more ingredients used in the casserole, the more you care about the family.

While there are some people in the South (funeral hoppers) who really only attend a funeral because they know they will get at least one meal and a snack out of their visitation, others can be grouped into one of three specific categories based on the food they bring to the grieving family's home: the funeral baker, the funeral buyer, and the funeral beggar.

The funeral baker, some might say, is the person who cares the most about the deceased. If she cares enough to cook for them, then she really does want to show how much she wants to help ease the family's grief. Baking takes time and effort. During this baking time, she is thinking of the family of the deceased and praying for them to heal quickly. She feels as if she is helping the family cope. The funeral baker can often show up late, but the excuse always falls back on the time spent baking the elaborate dish.

The funeral buyer stills cares very much for the deceased and his or her family. However, she feels she can offer more by giving her time and words. Or she could just really stink at baking, and rather than show up and embarrass herself with a terrible dish, she pays others to cook for her.

The funeral buyer relies heavily on delis, bakeries, and restaurants—usually local—and the item brought is the signature item of that business. The closer she feels to the family, the more expensive the dish she orders. There are benefits to being a funeral buyer: she is the first to arrive on the scene to offer sympathies (not that the family will ever remember), and if the food turns out to be terrible, she can blame it on the place where it was purchased.

The occasional funeral buyer likes to take risks and transfers the bought food to one of her own pieces of silver or china and then tries to pawn the dish off as if she had labored for hours in the kitchen. Most other guests can tell the difference, especially when the funeral buyer is questioned on ingredients and can't truthfully answer.

Finally, there are the funeral beggars. They are not beggars in the sense that they are begging for money or food or asking for a handout. They don't walk in with signs on their chests that read, "Will Grieve for Food." However, they are the type of beggars who show up with their favorite foods—usually fast food and more often than not a bucket of Kentucky Fried Chicken (with the beggars' favorite chicken pieces) or Pizza Hut pizzas (with the beggars' favorite toppings). They do this because the funeral beggars know they will be eating at least two of their meals at the grieving family's home, and they want to make sure they enjoy. The funeral beggars almost always leave with a "to-go" plate full of leftovers and have even been caught nabbing two or three or six cans of soda to take with them in case they get thirsty.

The funeral beggars really make it hard for the grieving family for a couple of reasons—especially when it comes time to write thank-you notes. There are often times when food listed on the "whom to thank for what" list was never even seen by the grieving family because it was taken by a beggar. Or the opposite—food seen by the grieving family was never added to the list.

In addition, funeral beggars don't attend a visitation alone; they bring

their sons and daughters, in-laws, cousins, and other extended family members plus all of *their* friends and family, who are just there for the food because they certainly didn't have a relationship with the deceased. By doing so, the beggars are adding extra work to the grief stricken when it is time to write thank-you notes. They can get carpal tunnel syndrome just from thanking the beggars' relatives and friends.

Funerals are, in a weird way, a time of celebrating the

wonderful life the deceased person led (even if it was not so wonderful). It is amazing that even at a crack dealer's funeral, people will discuss only the great things he or she did in life.

"Remember in first grade when he helped Granny across the street."

"Remember when she won the art contest in junior high."

You never really hear things like "Remember when he started selling crack across the street from the middle school right after he dropped out of high school." Or "Remember when she was suspended for carrying a gun to school and shooting a hole in the wall right after the art contest."

Nope, just the good stuff is talked about at both Southern funerals and Northern funerals.

It took a whole year of living in the North before I attended a funeral. An acquaintance of our family passed away, and I immediately went into action.

In this situation I was the classic funeral buyer, so I rushed to Giant (the North's version of Kroger—only bigger), straight to the deli section, and purchased a baked macaroni and cheese casserole and then headed to the bakery section for a cake.

I prodded my husband into going over to the house of the grieving with me by telling him about all of the food that would be there. He told me, "You are crazy. People don't take food when they visit the family. They don't even go to that person's house. They go to the funeral home."

He tagged along anyway for two reasons: to prove he was right and to get a good meal if I happened to be right. We drove to the family's home, and of course, it was pitch black inside. I didn't give up so easily. I tried the excuses: "Maybe they are grieving so hard they can't even stand to look at anybody. Maybe they are on their way home from somewhere."

Finally my husband allowed me to go and knock on the door to see if there was any way possible I could be right. I was wrong. No one was home. So we traveled back into town and drove by the funeral home. Lo and behold, it was packed with people. So many people that a line had formed outside of the building, all waiting to go in and greet the family.

We took our places in line, and the man in front of us turned around and said, "This is a lot of people for a viewing."

A viewing? I thought to myself. *What the heck is a viewing?* "Are we going to be watching a movie or something?" I asked my husband.

"Woman, what are you talking about?" he responded. "We are at a viewing."

"What do you mean exactly by 'viewing'?" I questioned.

"A viewing. You know, you go in, look at the body, hug the family, sign the book, and go home," he explained.

"What? Look at the body? I'm not looking at the body. I'm just going to hug the family and sign the book!" I stated frantically.

"You have to look at the body in order to get to the family. Haven't you ever been to a viewing before? What do you'uns do in the South?" my husband asked—again with the *you'uns*.

"I've been to a wake and to a visitation. Duh!" I exclaimed. "And it is an option whether or not we want to see the dead body. We are not forced to see a dead body like y'all are forcing me to do."

"Well it is not an option here. You have to look at the body. And by the way, you are the one who made me come to this viewing anyway," my husband said in an embarrassed tone.

It had become obvious to others in line that we were having a discussion about this dead body that we barely knew. There were many ears pointed in our direction while their whispers were headed in the opposite direction.

We finally entered the funeral home, signed the book, and stood in line again, waiting. Only this wait involved watching others as they passed by the body to offer the family their condolences. No one seemed to have a problem looking at the deceased, so I thought maybe I could handle it. I was at least going to give it a shot.

And then we moved closer and closer, and I felt my heart beating faster and faster. I wasn't going to be able to handle it after all. I thought I might have an anxiety attack just thinking about what to do once I reached the

dead body. *Do I talk to it? Do I smile at it? Do I touch it?* "No," I accidentally said out loud.

"Who are you talking to?" my husband asked.

"Sorry," I whimpered.

Then other, less rational, questions started forming in my head: *What
if his eyes open up? What if I accidentally knock the casket over and the
body falls out? What if he is not really dead?* I really could have used a
Valium.

As we moved closer to the front of the room, I noticed that next to the
casket were a bunch of flower arrangements. I thought, *Great! I will just
read all of the cards on the flower arrangements. It will look as if I am
looking at the body, but I will really just be reading and moving closer to
the family.*

So I did just that. I read how friends were sorry, wishing the family
their best, and offering sympathies. Each and every flower—plastic or
real—was analyzed by me while waiting in that line. *Whew! I made it.
Now I just have to be strong while greeting the family.*

We reached the mother of the deceased first. I went to hug her, and
she guided me right back to the casket and asked, "Doesn't he look
good? They did a real good job making him look like himself, didn't they?
Just look at him."

My heart was palpitating as fast as it does when I watch Johnny Depp
on the big screen . . . fast . . . only I usually don't get nauseous when
I'm watching Johnny Depp. So I said the only thing I thought a true
Southerner would say: "I brought you a cakerole. I mean a cake and a
casserole."

Lucky for me, casseroles and cakes were favorites of the deceased.
However, after leaving the viewing and starting to believe my husband
about how things work in the North, neither the casserole nor the cake
ever made it to the family. (Did I mention I eat when I'm stressed?)

I have since found out from my Northern friends that it is common to
take food to the family of the deceased . . . but just not as much as in

the South. And although the food I've seen during the visitations and viewings I've been to in both the North and the South are extremely different, they are all offered to show love and respect for the deceased. Well, most of them anyway.

Funeral food must be quick and easy. Sobbing while cooking is never a good combination, so you will see these recipes utilize some prepared items to speed up the process.

Four Cheese Garlic Grits

8 cups water
2 cups grits
1 stick butter
½ cup Parmesan cheese
½ cup Brie
¾ cup milk, half & half, or heavy cream

1 tablespoon salt
4 cloves chopped garlic
½ cup shredded cheddar cheese
½ cup Monterey Jack or Gruyere cheese
2 eggs lightly beaten

Preheat oven to 350 degrees. Bring the water to a boil and add salt. Whisk in grits (this will prevent lumps). Turn heat to low and occasionally stir until the grits are thick—about 10 minutes. Sauté the garlic in butter until fragrant. Add butter and garlic to the grits, stir in cheeses, and let them melt completely. Add milk and eggs, mixing well. Pour the mixture into a greased 9x13 casserole dish and bake for 45 minutes until the center is set.

Delivered by Angels
Asparagus & Egg Casserole

8 slices white bread, crust removed and cut into triangles
2 bunches asparagus, blanched and cut into bite-size pieces
10 eggs, lightly beaten
2 teaspoons Tony Chachere's Creole Seasoning
2 teaspoons Worcestershire sauce
1 teaspoon pepper

2 cups shredded Parmesan cheese
1 cup shredded mozzarella cheese
2 cups milk
1 tablespoon Dijon mustard
2 teaspoons salt

Cover the bottom of a greased 9x13 casserole dish with the bread triangles. Combine the cheeses and sprinkle over the bread, and then layer with the asparagus pieces. Mix together the remaining ingredients and pour over the layers. Refrigerate overnight, and bake at 375 degrees for 45 minutes. (You can also add cooked sausage and colored peppers to this dish.)

If you are taking this to a grieving family, cook it halfway at home and let them finish the cooking.
Under no circumstances do you take the casserole without it being cooked halfway.
It will slosh all over your car and the smell will never leave!

Sausage Pinwheels

1 sheet of puff pastry
1 pound uncooked ground sausage, mild
½ cup green onions, chopped
½ cup white cheddar cheese, grated

Preheat oven to 400 degrees. Spread the sausage over the puff pastry sheet leaving a one-inch border on all sides. Sprinkle the green onions and cheddar cheese on the top of the sausage. Roll the pastry like a jelly roll, starting with the widest side of the rectangle. Wrap in plastic wrap and chill for four hours. (At this point, it can be frozen, but thaw completely before proceeding with the recipe.) Slice the roll into half-inch slices. Place on a greased baking sheet. Brush with egg wash* and bake until golden and sausage is cooked through, about 30 minutes.

*Egg wash is one egg lightly beaten with 1 tablespoon water.

You can make these into a sweet treat by replacing the sausage, onions, and cheese with ½ cup sugar, ¼ cup cinnamon, and ½ cup raisins.

Better Than Counseling Curried Fruit

Do not pass up making this recipe, regardless of how revolting it might seem. It is wonderful and the perfect option for fruit in the winter.

1 can pears
1 can apricots
1 can seedless Bing cherries
1 cup brown sugar
2 teaspoons curry powder
½ cup sherry

1 can peaches
1 can pineapple chunks
3 tablespoons butter
½ teaspoon ground ginger
juice of one lemon
3 tablespoons brandy

Preheat oven to 325 degrees. Drain all cans of fruit well and cut the large pieces into chunks. Pour into a 3-quart casserole. Sauté the butter, brown sugar, ginger, curry powder, and lemon juice in a medium saucepan for 3-4 minutes. Pour over the fruit and mix well. Pour the sherry and brandy over the whole mixture. Cook for one hour.

Something to Gossip About Pork Tenderloin

This recipe, although somewhat expensive, is easy to prepare. Death doesn't give notice, so this will fit into the busiest of schedules.

1 1½-pound pork tenderloin
1 tablespoon Tony Chachere's Creole Seasoning

salt and pepper

Marinade

½ cup orange juice concentrate

½ cup soy sauce

Mix together marinade and add to the pork for a minimum of 2 hours up to overnight. Remove the tenderloin from the marinade and pat dry. Sprinkle with salt, pepper, and Creole Seasoning. Preheat oven to 350 degrees. Cook the tenderloin until it reaches 145 degrees internal temperature (around 30-35 minutes). Baste with juices 2 or 3 times during the cooking process to promote caramelization.

Orange Soy Sauce

1 18-ounce jar orange marmalade
1 teaspoon crushed red pepper flakes

¼ cup soy sauce
½ cup chicken broth

Mix all ingredients in a medium saucepan. Cook over medium heat and reduce by half. Serve with pork tenderloin or any other meat.

Comfort Your Soul Chicken, Artichoke, & Wild Rice Casserole

2 tablespoons butter
½ cup green onions, chopped
½ cup sherry
1 cup Hellmann's Mayonnaise
1 cup Parmesan cheese (2 tablespoons reserved)
3 cups cooked shredded chicken breast
2 cups cooked wild rice
One 10-ounce package frozen chopped spinach, thawed
        (make sure to squeeze out extra liquid)

8 ounces chopped mushrooms
1 clove garlic, chopped
1 can of cream of . . . *
½ cup sour cream
½ cup Swiss cheese (2 tablespoons reserved)
salt and pepper
1 14-ounce can artichoke hearts, drained

Melt butter over medium heat in a sauté pan and cook mushrooms, green onions, and garlic until the mushrooms release their liquid and become soft. Set aside to cool. In a medium mixing bowl, mix sherry, soup, mayonnaise, sour cream, and cheeses. Add the cooled mushroom mixture and chicken. Taste and add salt and pepper as needed.

In a 9x13 casserole dish, spread the wild rice across the bottom and layer with artichoke hearts then spinach. Pour the mayonnaise mixture over the top and sprinkle with reserved cheeses. Bake at 350 degrees for 35-45 minutes.

*Can of cream of . . . * refers to cream of mushroom, cream of celery, or cream of chicken soups. I personally don't use the cream of chicken because its mechanically separated chicken parts scare me.*

Marinated Vegetables

These vegetables are a welcome sight when you have eaten so much unhealthy comfort food that it's likely you will be the next one in the casket. Always err on the side of undercooking the veggies while blanching then plunge them into an ice bath to stop cooking.

1 pint grape tomatoes
1 can artichoke hearts, drained and quartered
1 cup green beans, blanched

1 red pepper
1 bunch asparagus, blanched
2 cucumbers, peeled and sliced

Marinade

1 tablespoon Dijon mustard
3 tablespoons Hellmann's Mayonnaise
1 cup olive oil

½ cup lemon juice
3 cloves garlic, chopped
salt and pepper

In the bowl of a food processor, add mustard, lemon juice, mayonnaise, and garlic and pulse three times. Then, with the motor running, drizzle the olive oil in until it thickens. Add salt and pepper to taste. If it gets too thick, add a couple of tablespoons of water. Adding more oil only continues to thicken the mixture. Toss the vegetables in the marinade and refrigerate for at least 1 hour up to 4 hours.

Chocolate Chip Bundt Cake

This recipe makes two Bundt cakes, so you can take one to the grieving family and one to the family you forgot was grieving two months ago. Better late than never.

2 boxes yellow cake mix
4 3.4-ounce instant Jell-O chocolate pudding mixes
8 eggs, beaten

1 cup vegetable oil
1 cup water
24 ounces chocolate chips

Preheat oven to 350 degrees. In a stand mixer with a paddle attachment, mix all ingredients except the chocolate chips for 3 minutes. Fold in the chocolate chips and pour into 2 greased Bundt pans. Bake for 50–60 minutes until a knife inserted in the center comes out clean.

Coconut Glop Cake

The glop in this recipe is sheer genius! This cake is always the star at the Heiskell Easter picnic. Regardless of where the event will be held, the first question asked when the planning begins is "Who is bringing the glop cake?"

Cake: 1 Duncan Hines butter cake mix, made as directed on the box in two 8-inch round cake pans. Split each layer into two layers by slicing horizontally. You should have 4 layers.

Glop: Mix together 2 cups sugar, 8 ounces sour cream, and 12 ounces shredded coconut and refrigerate for 2 hours. Stir and take out 1 cup to reserve for the icing. Place the glop between the layers of the cake.

Icing: Mix together 1 cup of glop and 2 cups Cool Whip. Cover the cake with icing and store in the refrigerator for at least 24 hours. Can be held in the refrigerator for up to 2 days.

Bridal Showers

Save the Date Sun-Dried Tomato BLTs
Sorta Kinda Like Merigold Tomatoes
Crab and Brie Soup
Chicken and Spinach Crepes
Chocolate Covered Strawberries
Chocolate Snowballs

Chapter Five
SHE'S GETTING MARRIED . . . PASS THE TOILET PAPER

Southern Bridal Shower, n.: A special time where you can use the fine china and shower the bride-to-be with personalized gifts—especially if this is the bride's first marriage.

"Surprise!" we yelled as my co-worker walked into the restaurant where her bridal shower was being held.

"What's with all the toilet paper?" she asked, looking around the room. I had asked myself this same question one hundred times before she arrived. Each table had a centerpiece and several rolls of toilet paper. *This will definitely be different from a Southern bridal shower*, I thought to myself. *I just hope I don't embarrass myself.*

"Just sit down and have a drink," the mother of the honoree shouted.

After that statement I thought maybe it *would* be a little like a Southern bridal shower. I didn't order a drink at this shower. I am not much of a risk taker, and since I had no clue as to what we were supposed to do with the toilet paper, I wasn't going to take any chances.

We took time to mingle and hug the bride and tell her how gorgeous she will be at her wedding. We discussed things like whether or not her tattoo would be hidden by her wedding dress, whether or not the men would wear camouflaged bow ties, and where the couple would spend their honeymoon.

And then we began the first game—wrapping the bride in toilet paper, like a mummy. This was a timed event to be completed by groups of three. I didn't know anyone on my team, and when one woman took a leadership position by directing us how to wrap the toilet paper the fastest, I knew we were in trouble. I sometimes have trouble with authority, and even if the authority is right, I might try to come up with a different solution. However, I am also a great team player. So I ran circles around the bride with my toilet paper roll between my two index fingers while being followed by my teammates doing the same thing. I was dizzy and a little nauseous, but I didn't give up. We wrapped the bride in seven minutes flat. Then it was the other team's turn. Their method was for one person to stand in front of the bride and, because she was skinny, wrap the toilet paper around her from head to toe. My team lost.

I'm a very competitive person, so when they said, "Time for the next game, get your roll of toilet paper," it was on. Game time. And it was a solo game, so I thought I had it in the bag. We were instructed to pull off as many squares of toilet paper that we thought were necessary to win the game. The girls in front of me pulled off five and six. I thought, *I'm definitely going to beat them.* I pulled off twenty-three squares. Everyone started laughing, including myself, acting like I knew what was going on. Apparently I was the only one who didn't know the game. Turns out we had to list at least one thing we knew about the bride on each square of toilet paper. I had only known her for about a month. So of course, I lost again.

My desire to win was increasing with each minute. Between ordering our food and opening gifts, we had one final game to play with the toilet paper: the toilet paper dash, where you put a square of toilet paper on the tip of your nose and race your opponent to the opposite end of the room. I didn't care how stupid I looked—a grown woman running around the back room of a restaurant with toilet paper on the tip of her nose—I wanted to win.

"On your mark, get set, go!"

I took off faster than a bullet leaving a gun on the first day of deer season. I was in the race for about three seconds. You can imagine my disappointment and total embarrassment when I tripped over an air bubble that seemed to just pop up under the carpet as I ran by. I went toilet-paper-covered nose first into the faded and worn maroon fibers of the dirty carpet. Laughter erupted throughout the room, and my face turned the color of a ripe tomato. My shoes flew off my feet only to uncover my toes sticking through holes in the stockings. The redness in my face glowed with each gasp made between laughs. I couldn't help but join in on the laughter, especially when the mother of the bride yelled, "Pass the toilet paper, I've got to blow my nose."

I guess all the excitement—or maybe the dust that flew up from the rug when I fell—ignited her allergies, and she used the rest of her toilet paper roll to clear her passages. What a great day that turned out to be. It was full of laughter, games, and hardly any gossip. The gifts given were practical, and not one thing was engraved or monogrammed. It was not at all what I was used to seeing at a Southern bridal shower.

In the South the only time you would see toilet paper at a bridal shower is when you went to powder your nose in the ladies' room (unless one of the guests forgot to triple check herself in the mirror on the way out and had a few squares sticking out of her skirt or on the bottom of her designer shoes.)

Bridal showers in the South are sometimes quite serious. There are games and laughter, but much more conservative than at a Northern bridal shower. All of the wild times are saved for the bachelorette party. The bridal shower is more formal and is planned to impress rather than entertain. While entertainment definitely takes place, it is an organized entertainment, evading too much spontaneity. But if beauty is what you want, a Southern bridal shower is the place to go.

No matter where the shower is held, you can count on fresh flowers that look as if they were delivered from the pages of a magazine and food so perfect, it almost looks fake. Everything is placed in or on a silver container—sterling—usually engraved with the family crest.

Everyone is dressed up, and the gifts are flawlessly wrapped, waiting to be opened by the bride. The neatly arranged bows on top will be carefully removed, because it is a Southern wives' tale that the number of bows broken during the opening of gifts equates to how many children the bride and her new groom will create. To avoid overpopulating the Southern half of the United States, the bows are gently removed and carefully bundled into a bouquet that will be tucked away in a box for years to come.

Usually, only positive discussions are held—whether the information provided in those conversations is true or not. Compliments float around the room and often bump into one another depending on how long it has been since two people united last. The bride is discussed in full detail—what dress she will be wearing and where she bought it (which in a way implies the cost of the dress without having to actually say the cost). If you are having your dress "made," then you are not paying very much. However, if you are having your dress "custom-made," then you are paying way more than anyone should pay for a one-time-wear dress. But just because you might not pay a lot for a dress, it doesn't mean the wedding will be cheap.

There are many ways to tell how expensive a girl's wedding will be, and all of these topics are discussed at the bridal shower. For example, does she have a wedding planner? In hiring a wedding planner, the bride implies that the wedding will be so extensive and expensive that she and her mother cannot handle all of the details themselves because it would be too overwhelming. A wedding planner is needed to help you organize, get quotes from the best of the best at everything, and then help you make your final decision (which will always be top price). If you are not using a wedding planner, you are somewhat more practical and want to keep an eye on the budget. It may even mean you are paying for some of the wedding yourself—also a rare occasion in the South (at least in my experiences).

In the South, wedding planning starts the day after the birth of a little girl. Every boy met throughout the girl's life is greeted with a wide eye in case he could be the one, the lucky one. Each piece of estate jewelry purchased is a potential engagement ring. That is, when the groom-to-be is not as experienced in the jewelry department.

Picking out a wedding dress starts soon after high school graduation. Even if it takes ten more years to find the groom, the dress needs to be decided upon early so that there will be one less dispute when the big day arrives.

The location of the wedding reception is also a very telling way to discover the price of the wedding. Getting married in a local church does not cost much, but the reception could cost a lot. A destination wedding costs a little more only because you have to pay to use the facilities of others. However, you are only inviting close friends and family, so prices of the food and drinks go down.

If you are having a wedding reception in the backyard of your home or someone else's home, you can count on it being expensive. Having a home-based wedding reception can mean great things: tents, ice sculptures, catered buffets, and even some moderate remodeling on the inside of the home. What better excuse to have new flooring installed or to have the interior repainted?

What type of music will be playing at the reception will also let you know how much a bride is spending on her wedding. If she is having

DJ Danny Joe, then it is probably only costing a couple thousand dollars. However, if the area's most famous local live band is showing up to play, she is putting down some money to rent them for the evening. This also means the party will be more lively and will last well into the moonlit hours.

The cake, the money teller of all money tellers, is a topic that is discussed at every Southern bridal shower. The more tiers it has, the more money she spent. The more decorative it becomes, the more money it costs.

So you see, going to a Southern bridal shower is not just for gift-giving and entertainment, it is also educational. There is some serious math taking place among the guests of the shower—all trying to add and subtract just to find out how much this Southern bride's parents paid for her to get married. And all these costs are for the first marriage. God forbid there need to be a second.

Whether you attend a Southern bridal shower or a Northern bridal shower, just take these pieces of advice with you: let the bride have her day, don't try to make an over-the-top toast, and always remember the toilet paper.

Save the Date Sun-Dried Tomato BLTs

These are wonderful during the winter when tomatoes are not in season. Makes about 2 dozen.

1½ pounds bacon
1 cup Hellmann's Mayonnaise
2 cups fresh basil, chopped

4 ounces sun-dried tomatoes (NOT packed in oil)
1 loaf white bread

Cook all of the bacon. Let it cool and then crumble. Set aside.

Heat 3 cups of water in a small saucepan. Place the sun-dried tomatoes in a small bowl and cover with the hot water. Allow the tomatoes to soak until soft, about 15 minutes. Drain tomatoes and pat dry. Finely chop the tomatoes and set aside. Using a round biscuit cutter, make 2 dozen rounds out of the loaf of bread. Mix the tomatoes with mayonnaise. Spread each round with the tomato and mayonnaise mixture. Generously sprinkle the rounds with the crumbled bacon. Sprinkle the basil on top.

Sorta Kinda Like Merigold Tomatoes

McCartys Pottery is a true Southern institution located in Merigold, Mississippi. They have a lovely lunch place and serve these wonderful tomatoes. The McCarty family has held on to this recipe for years, and they aren't giving it up anytime soon. This is my rendition of their classic.

3 28-ounce cans of whole tomatoes, peeled and drained
½ cup fresh basil, chopped
1½ teaspoons salt
1½ cups grated Parmesan cheese
4 cups fresh bread crumbs

½ cup fresh spinach, chopped
1 tablespoon lemon zest
1 teaspoon pepper
1 tablespoon brown sugar
2 tablespoons melted butter

Mix together the tomatoes, spinach, basil, lemon zest, salt, pepper, and cheese and pour into a greased 9x13 casserole dish. Mix the brown sugar, bread crumbs, and melted butter together and top the tomato mixture. Bake at 350 degrees for 45 minutes.

Crab & Brie Soup

This recipe is from one of my favorite menus at Viking Cooking School.

Stock

½ cup clam juice
1 cup water
½ onion, quartered
½ stalk celery
2 cloves garlic, whole
½ cup white wine
1 bouquet garni consisting of 1 bay leaf, 4 peppercorns, 1 stem thyme, and 1 stem parsley
½ lemon, squeezed and added to pot

Combine all ingredients in a medium pot and simmer for 1 hour, then strain.

Soup

2 tablespoons butter
3 tablespoons flour
½ cup milk
½ cup heavy cream
⅛ teaspoon cayenne pepper
salt and pepper to taste
6 ounces Brie
4 ounces crabmeat
¼ cup sherry

Melt butter and whisk in flour. Cook over medium heat for 3-4 minutes. Add milk, heavy cream, spices, and stock and whisk to incorporate. Bring to a simmer and add the Brie. Once the Brie has melted, fold in the crabmeat. Add the sherry and serve immediately. Note: The stock and soup base (everything except the brie, crabmeat, and sherry) can be made 2-3 days in advance and refrigerated. Bring it to a simmer and add Brie, crab, and sherry, then serve immediately.

Pass in beautiful demitasse cups as guests arrive.

Chicken & Spinach Crepes

Try to make your crepes the week before and freeze them. It makes this process simpler. Makes 6 servings.

1 pound fresh spinach
8 ounces fresh mushrooms, sliced
salt and pepper
1 cup chicken broth
2 tablespoons cooking oil
3½ cups cooked chicken, shredded
12 crepes (recipe below)

10 tablespoons butter, divided
½ cup all-purpose flour
2 cups milk
1½ cups shredded white cheddar cheese
½ cup onion, chopped
½ teaspoon finely chopped lemon peel

Wash fresh spinach and remove stems. In a 3-quart saucepan, cook spinach in boiling salted water for 5 minutes. Drain and squeeze out excess water. Chop spinach and set aside.

For the sauce, heat 2 tablespoons butter. Add mushrooms and cook over medium-high heat until tender. Remove from heat and set aside. In a separate saucepan, melt 4 tablespoons butter and add flour, salt, and pepper to taste. Add milk and chicken broth. Cook and stir over medium heat until thick. Stir in 1 cup of the cheese until melted. Add in mushrooms, remove from heat, and set aside. For the filling, melt the remaining 4 tablespoons of butter in a 12-inch skillet and add the cooking oil. Add onion and cook over medium heat until tender. Stir in chicken, spinach, and 1 cup of the sauce and season with salt and the lemon peel.

Preheat oven to 350 degrees. Spoon ½ cup of the filling down the center of the unbrowned side of each crepe. Roll up crepes and place seam side down in a buttered 9x13 casserole dish. Spread the remaining sauce over the top and sprinkle with the remaining cheese. Bake for 30 minutes or until heated through and the top is lightly browned.

Crepes

1½ cups milk
2 eggs
¼ teaspoon salt

1 cup all-purpose flour
1 tablespoon vegetable oil

Combine all ingredients in a bowl and beat with a rotary beater until well mixed. Lightly grease a skillet and heat at medium heat. Remove from heat and spoon in 2 tablespoons of the mixture. Tilt the skillet in order to spread the batter. Return the skillet to the heat and brown the batter on one side. Flip the finished crepe onto a paper towel. Repeat with remaining batter, occasionally re-greasing skillet.

Chocolate Covered Strawberries

It's fun to drizzle some melted white chocolate over the hardened chocolate strawberries.

12 ounces bittersweet chocolate

1 large container strawberries, cleaned and dried

Melt chocolate in microwave, stopping often to stir. Dip the dried strawberries into the melted chocolate and let rest on wax paper until hard. Refrigerate until serving.

Chocolate Snowballs

These are wonderful to serve for winter showers. It's also nice to roll them in different types of crushed candy like M&M's, Oreos, and Reese's Peanut Butter Cups. Makes about 2 dozen balls.

1 cup heavy cream
1½ tablespoons brandy or other liqueur

10 ounces bittersweet chocolate, small pieces
3 cups shredded coconut

Pour the cream into a saucepan and bring to a boil over medium-high heat. Remove from heat and add the chocolate, stirring until melted. Add in brandy. Pour this mixture into a shallow, rimmed baking pan, cover and chill for at least 4 hours. Using a melon baller with a spring handle, scoop out balls of chocolate, and then roll them in the shredded coconut. Press hard enough for the coconut to adhere to the chocolate balls. Refrigerate until serving.

Baby Showers

Cheese Pennies
Eat for Two Apricot Walnut Chicken Salad in Butter Lettuce Cups
Bacon Bites
Gazpacho
French Pregtinis
How Sweet It Is Shrimp Salad in Toast Cups
Tomato Basil Tarts
Keep Your Figure Fresh Fruit Salad with Mint Syrup
Petite Tarts with Lime or Chocolate

Chapter Six

A Double-Wide Is a Perfect Place for a Baby Shower

Southern Baby Shower, n.: A wonderful time filled with gifts, great food, and great company . . . and hopefully it never takes place before the bridal shower.

Oh my goodness, do we ever love to throw a baby shower in the South. At almost every shower, you are sure to find some of the same staples: pecans, punch, petit fours, and a lot of presents. Champagne, Bloody Marys, and flavored homemade tea rest next to the silver platters filled with fancy finger foods. You have your choice of triangle shaped sandwiches, fresh fruit, and pasta salad sitting atop the greenest lettuce. An elaborately decorated and costly cake resides in the middle of the buffet and is considered a piece of art until the mother-to-be is ready to indulge.

One by one the guests arrive, beautifully wrapped gifts in tow, and smiles from ear to ear—even if they aren't that crazy about the guest of honor or some fellow attendees. No one dares to miss the event, and some people arrive even though they weren't officially invited. Baby showers in the Mississippi Delta can sometimes make the local newspaper, or better yet, the area magazine. Therefore, women in attendance want to make sure they have a fantastic outfit, matching shoes, and at least one piece of gossip tucked away in a special place just in case there is a need for it.

Compliments swirl through the room—just as they do at any other kind of shower—like a tornado in a hot summer storm (and filled with just as much debris).

"You look so good. Who did your hair? Where did you get your outfit? How's your mama doing?" These are just a few of the lies, I mean quotes, that start out some of the conversations heard at a baby shower as guests enter. They are followed up with hugs and brief "catch-me-ups" that allow attendees to quickly tell what has been going on in their lives over the past few months.

"Y'all take care now. Please come by and see us. Tell your mama and them we said 'Hey,'" are the conversation enders—words that take a guest from one set of women to the next, just to start all over again, "Hey! It's been so long since I've seen you. You look so good." And this continues until the rounds have been made and everyone has greeted each other.

Then it is time to eat—nibble, I mean. No one dares attend a Southern baby shower and eat more than a couple of bites of each item on display. Itsy-bitsy bites. Mainly because it is considered impolite to overeat at a shower, even though each and every woman there would like to take a nose dive into the cupcakes or the fancy-shaped miniature sandwiches. Each woman claims to be on a diet or about to be on a diet, but the truth is that each and every woman would sample every item twelve times if no one else was in the room. But they don't because they know they would be at the top of the gossip chain the next day. So instead, they eat small bites at the shower and then hit the fast-food drive-through on the way home.

Everyone feels the soon-to-be mother's belly, puts their bets down on what the name and sex of the baby will be, and then gravitates to the spot where they will watch the gifts opened. Then the opening begins—the main event. The soon-to-be grandmother is usually sitting next to the mother-to-be and keeping track of all the gifts so that she can later help her daughter write the perfect thank-you note for every single item received that day. Some of the most amazing, practical, and not-so-practical gifts are given at a Southern baby shower. Gifts are sometimes chosen to impress the other guests just as much to impress the recipient. So creativity and great wrapping are key components in gift giving.

One by one, the baby mama carefully unwraps each gift, places the wrapping in a large trash bag, then shrieks, "We need this so much! This is great. Thank you. THANK YOU!"

Then it is on to the next gift, and the same thing occurs over and over until she finally gets to the gift she has been dying to open all day. The one gift from that really rich friend or family member who always over-spends no matter what the occasion. It would kill her to allow the glory to go to some other present, and this is just fine with the guest of honor. This rich lady is invited to every party in town—and it is not because of her personality, rather her pocketbook. Yes, she is a sweet lady, a great friend and all that. Not great enough to know your true closet skeletons . . . but definitely great enough to befriend on a more superficial level.

She is the one who talks and walks just a little bit different than the others. She is the one who thinks she is a little bit better than all the others (and she may be). She is the one who demands more attention than the mom-to-be, even though she doesn't realize she is doing so. Her gift is opened more delicately than all the others; it is treated with great respect. There are no shrieks involved when this gift is unveiled. Instead, it is complete silence by the recipient. The gift has left her speechless. A small tear finds its way down the puffed up cheek of the mother-to-be as she whimpers, "I have always wanted this. I registered for it and didn't think I would ever get it."

And then the rest of us think to ourselves, *I didn't know she was registered anywhere.*

We realized at that moment that even the mom-to-be does not have enough confidence in us that we would or could get her a tear-invoking gift—so little confidence that she didn't even bother to tell us where she was registered. Her expectations of us were set at a gift from Walmart, and that is exactly what she ended up getting. Her expectations of us were that we would provide the "practical" gifts while her supposed wealthier friends would supply the gifts she really wanted. Unfortunately, we met her expectations, even though we could have easily gotten her a gift for which she registered.

The rich woman's generosity is complimented by the mother-to-be the rest of the day until finally she gets in her Mercedes and drives away — making all of us other, more "practical" gift givers seem cheap and unwanted. But that's okay, because there is always a Sonic Drive-In to drown our sorrows in just around the corner. (And with all the money we didn't spend on a gift, we can even get the combo.)

The hostess of the shower ensures that drinks are refilled and the magnificently catered buffet is stocked. There is no time for game playing at a Southern baby shower. Everyone leaves immediately after gifts are opened, even the mother-to-be, without her gifts. Those are left for her husband to pick up later in his Chevy truck.

One of the most fun, most relaxed showers I've been to was in the North. The shower was for the girlfriend of a friend of my husband. I did not really know this girl and had no idea why I even attended, except that

I was longing for the excitement you can get from watching someone open gifts.

I was warned in advance not to dress up, so of course, I wore dress slacks and a sweater set, just in case no one else abided by those rules. That happens sometimes in the South. Even when you tell guests not to dress up, they still take that opportunity to wear their brand new sundress or to show off their name-brand pumps. I quickly learned that is not the case in the North. Flannel shirts and jeans were worn by almost everyone in attendance, unless a sweatshirt better suited them.

So I traveled way out in the country, around many mountain roads, following the directions to the baby shower, and ended at a double-wide mobile home (under construction). I parked in the yard, and my heels sunk in the mud with each step I took toward the party.

"I told you not to dress up," yelled the mother-to-be.

"I should have listened," I responded, juggling my gifts.

I passed through the smoking section on the deck (where several women were complaining about their husbands), spoke to the mother-to-be, and headed into the kitchen where I placed my casserole dish—which had been requested by the mom-to-be. It was a potluck shower that started just around suppertime. The kitchen was full of delicious homemade foods. From spaghetti, franks and beans, baked macaroni, hamburgers, and hot dogs to brownies and chips—it was there. Crock pots lined the counter-tops and were filled with delicious homemade meals. And I don't mean homemade like when I make something at home from a box and call it homemade. I mean original recipe, made from scratch, homemade foods. Comfort foods at their finest. And boy did I get comforted that evening.

I tried to be polite, as if at a Southern baby shower, and took one spoonful of each item to taste. And then I was told I was being rude by not eating more. That's all I needed to hear to get in line for the second time and fill my plate with some great food.

After feasting, it was game time. I was shocked to hear we were going to play games. I was ready to go home, change into some stretchable, comfortable clothing, and watch television. It had already been over an hour since I arrived, so I was expecting to only be there for the gift opening. But I stayed and was in for a complete shock. All I can say is the name of the game was "Guess the Poop," and it involved candy bars and diapers. While I was floored by the nature of the game, I had never laughed so hard at a baby shower. I had been so accustomed to conservative showers — just opening the gifts and laughing only if the mom-to-be thought the joke was funny too. I caught myself several times at this Northern shower looking around to make sure I was not the only one really enjoying myself. I think I was drunk off all the food and laughter that had been served.

The mom-to-be was asked on several occasions, "Where is your sister?"

"I didn't invite her," she responded. "We're fighting."

Inside I gasped loudly and quickly thought to myself, *How could she not invite her own sister? Oh my goodness. There will be a family feud for sure. She really embarrassed her family by doing this.* And then it hit me, *Maybe this is the right way of doing things.* In the South, even if the fight of the century is going on, we invite that person and she shows up — even if just for that day. It would be worse not to show up and ruin the happy family image than to show up and fake it for a day.

Three hours of games and laughter had me exhausted. I left the party happy, full, and thinking if we could add a little bit of Northern excitement to the elegance of a Southern baby shower, we would have an all-time, for-the-record-books, perfect event.

The days when being pregnant meant you wore a tent and stayed at home are over. Pregnant Southern women are chic and stylish. Their baby shower should be no different. Think beyond the pink or blue box and make sure the mother's personality shines through in all aspects of the shower.

Cheese Pennies

½ cup butter, softened
1 pound sharp cheddar cheese, finely grated
1 teaspoon salt
¼ teaspoon cayenne pepper

½ cup shortening
2½ cups flour
1 teaspoon dry mustard

Using a stand mixer with a paddle attachment, beat the butter and shortening, then beat in the cheese. Add the dry ingredients and beat until well mixed. Transfer the dough to a clean surface. Shape the dough into a log about 2 inches wide. Wrap dough in plastic wrap and place in the refrigerator until chilled, about 4 hours.

Preheat oven to 350 degrees. Remove the plastic wrap and slice the cheese log into ¼ inch slices. Bake on a cookie sheet until golden brown, about 15 minutes. Makes 8-10 dozen.

Eat for Two Apricot Walnut Chicken Salad in Butter Lettuce Cups

5 cups cooked chicken, shredded
¼ cup canned apricots, drained, chopped
2 tablespoons juice from apricot packing
1 cup Hellmann's Mayonnaise
    (don't even think about another brand)

¼ cup chopped dried apricots
¼ cup chopped walnuts
¼ cup chopped celery
1 tablespoon Greek seasoning
1 head Bibb or Boston lettuce

Mix all ingredients except lettuce. Allow salad to sit for a few hours to let the flavors meld. For a pretty presentation, use the natural cup made by the lettuce leaf to serve the chicken salad.

To cook proper chicken salad, only use bone-in, skin-on chicken breast. Dark meat is vulgar in chicken salad. Simmer the chicken breast in salted water with a chopped whole onion, 2 bay leaves, 4 celery tops, and 10 peppercorns. Once the chicken is cooked through, leave it in the water to cool, which will help keep the meat tender. Once cool enough to handle, drain water, reserving 2 tablespoons of stock. After removing the meat from the skin and bones, shred and toss with reserved stock and proceed with the recipe.

Bacon Bites

This is, by far, my most sought-after recipe . . . so here it is in all its glory!

1 box very thin breadsticks
1 package Oscar Mayer bacon
2 cups brown sugar

Preheat oven to 350 degrees. Spread the brown sugar onto a plate. Wrap the bacon starting at one end of the breadstick, barely overlapping, and then roll the bacon-covered breadstick in the brown sugar, pressing it to adhere. (At this point, you can refrigerate overnight.) Place the breadsticks on a foil-lined baking sheet and bake until bacon is cooked and almost crisp, about 45 minutes. Once done, remove sticks from baking sheet while warm or they will stick like glue. Place on wax paper to come to room temperature.

Gazpacho

Don't even bother with this soup if tomatoes are out of season. Just wait — it will be that much better, and you will enjoy it ten times more.

3 ripe tomatoes
⅓ cup sweet onions, finely chopped
⅓ cup green peppers, finely chopped
½ cup cucumber, peeled and chopped
2 teaspoons salt
3 cloves garlic, chopped
¼ teaspoon white pepper
½ teaspoon Tabasco
2 teaspoons Worcestershire sauce
4 tablespoons olive oil
2 tablespoons lemon juice
1½ cups V8 juice

Place all ingredients except the V8 juice in a food processor. Once the vegetables are finely chopped, add the juice. Continue to process until smooth. Taste and adjust seasonings. Serve chilled.

Pass this soup at a baby shower in silver baby cups for a beautiful effect.

French Pregtinis

4 cups pineapple juice
1 cup orange juice
4 cups ginger ale

2 cups cranberry juice
½ cup apricot nectar

Mix and serve in martini glasses and float fresh raspberries in the glass.

It is fun to rim the glasses with colored sugar: pink for a baby girl and light blue for a baby boy. Use just a drop of food coloring to tint the sugar. Place 2 tablespoons of orange juice on a plate. Invert the martini glass and dip into the juice, then barely dip the rim into the sugar and turn right side up.

How Sweet It Is Shrimp Salad
in Toast Cups

2 pounds cooked shrimp, peeled and deveined
½ cup Hellmann's Mayonnaise
⅛ teaspoon Zatarain's Liquid Crab Boil
¼ cup celery, finely diced
¼ cup cucumbers, peeled and finely diced
salt and pepper to taste

Cut shrimp into 1-inch pieces. Mix with all other ingredients. Chill until ready to use.

Toast Cups

1 loaf white bread
1 stick of salted butter, melted

Preheat oven to 300 degrees. Using a large biscuit cutter, cut bread rounds from the sliced bread. Brush both sides of the bread with the melted butter. Press each piece into a muffin cup and cook until they are completely dry throughout. If they do not get completely dry, they will not be crisp once they cool.

Tomato Basil Tart

This is not a pizza—that is why we go light on the cheese. The cheese is only there to hold the tomatoes in place.

1 sheet puff pastry
2 teaspoons kosher salt
6 small ripe tomatoes, sliced thin
¾ cup freshly grated Parmesan cheese

3 tablespoons olive oil
½ teaspoon pepper
¼ cup mozzarella cheese
1 cup fresh basil, chopped

Preheat oven to 400 degrees. Place the pastry sheet on a rimmed baking sheet, prick dough with a fork very well. Bake until halfway done, about 7-10 minutes. Remove from the oven. If the pastry puffs up like a pillow during the pre-bake, just press it down and continue. Brush with olive oil, sprinkle with salt and pepper, and layer the tomatoes, then the cheeses. Put the tart back into the oven and cook until cheese melts and pastry is cooked, about 15-20 minutes. Remove from oven and sprinkle with fresh basil. Cut into squares and serve while still warm.

Keep Your Figure Fresh Fruit Salad with Mint Syrup

1 cup sugar
1 cup fresh mint
1 honeydew melon, cut with a melon baller
1 baby watermelon, cut with melon baller
1 cantaloupe, cut with a melon baller
1 can mandarin oranges, drained

1 cup water
1 pint raspberries
1 pint blueberries
1 pint blackberries
1 can pineapple, drained

Make a simple syrup by bringing water and sugar to a boil. Once the sugar dissolves, add the mint and let it steep until it cools, then strain. Discard the mint. Cover all of the fruit with the syrup and serve. To garnish, top with chopped fresh mint. For a nice change, add 2 tablespoons of good bourbon to the simple syrup. After you mix the fruit with the simple syrup, dust with powdered sugar for a mint julep fruit salad.

This is also attractive on skewers. Alternate fruit with mint leaves.
Thinly sliced prosciutto ribbons on the skewer with the fruit is also lovely.

Petite Tarts with Lime or Chocolate

Pastry Shells

1 cup flour
1 stick butter, room temperature

4 ounces cream cheese, room temperature

Preheat oven to 350 degrees. In a stand mixer, mix the ingredients until thoroughly combined. Shape dough into a disc and wrap in plastic. Chill for 2 hours. Remove plastic. Pinch off a piece of dough about an inch and a half in diameter. Using your thumb, press the small piece into a mini muffin pan, making sure to bring the pastry up the sides of cup. Bake until golden brown, about 12-15 minutes.

Lime Filling

1 tub Cool Whip
7 ounces sweetened condensed milk

1 12-ounce can frozen limeade concentrate
3 tablespoons lime zest

Mix all ingredients and place a teaspoon into each pastry shell. Garnish with more zest or a fresh blueberry.

Chocolate Filling

½ cup heavy cream
1 tablespoon butter

12 ounces chocolate chips
1 teaspoon brandy

Bring heavy cream to a simmer over medium heat. Remove from heat and add chocolate chips. Stir until melted. Whisk in butter and brandy. Put filling in the refrigerator to allow it to harden. Fill the tarts with the chocolate mixture and top with a dollop of freshly whipped cream* and fresh strawberry slice.

* To whip heavy cream in a stand mixer fitted with a whisk attachment, mix 1 cup heavy cream, 3 tablespoons powdered sugar, and 1 teaspoon vanilla and whip until stiff peaks form. If you are so inclined, a little bourbon helps to round out the whipped cream and complements the chocolate.

Thanksgiving

Delta Roasted Turkey with Million Dollar Gravy
Call Me Southern Cornbread Dressing
Somebody Put Sweet Potatoes in My Orange Cups
This Ain't from a Can Cranberry Sauce
Oysters Osceola
Asparagus with Shallot Butter
Parmesan Mashed Potatoes
He's Gone Hunting Horseradish Mashed Potatoes
The Girls Stayed Home Grand Mimosas

Chapter Seven
Somebody Stole the Cornbread from My Dressing

Southern Thanksgiving, n.: A holiday soaked in the tradition of gathering with family, giving thanks, and an all-out competition of who can eat the most without having to take an afternoon nap.

My first Thanksgiving in Pennsylvania started out sad. I had been living outside of the state of Mississippi for only eleven months and had been hoping to return for the holidays. However, it wasn't meant to be, and my new husband and I would spend our first Thanksgiving together with his family. The good news was that my parents were on their way up to Pennsylvania for the holidays. So even though I couldn't be in the South, I would still be with them.

I only eat dressing once or twice a year. I have no idea how to make it (unless it is from the one-step Stove Top box), so at both Thanksgiving and Christmas, I try to savor my time with homemade dressing. My first Thanksgiving in Pennsylvania would test both my patience and my mental stability.

We joined a family feast in progress, and there it was—the dressing. I stared at it as if I had reunited with a long lost, yet not forgotten, love. It looked so perfect just sitting there. It was a golden brown on top and smelled like heaven.

"Would you like some of that stuffing?" my husband asked, laughing at me.

"No. I want some of that dressing," I responded.

We sat down and filled our plates. I sprinkled mine with turkey, peas, and corn, and then put a huge spoonful of dressing in the middle of my plate—like a centerpiece of art. We said a prayer and began to eat.

I scooped some dressing onto my fork and gently placed it in my mouth, wanting to savor that first bite as I do every year at Thanksgiving. But this year, something was different. Something was missing. My eyes widened as I continued to taste this Northern dressing, trying to figure out what had happened and why my palate was not completely satisfied. I was shocked and stunned. I thought to myself, *Somebody stole the corn-bread from my dressing.*

The cornbread was missing. It was gone. *What happened to it? Should I say something? Maybe they don't know it is missing.* All I tasted was bread. It was delicious, yes, but definitely not what I was expecting—which was the fabulous grittiness of the cornbread and seasonings in Southern-style dressing. I washed it down with some water and a spoonful of the baked corn casserole (my new favorite way to eat corn) and sat for a while before continuing. I needed time to digest—not the food—but the idea of dressing without cornbread.

And then I was passed these oversized balls of dough and vegeta-bles called "filling balls" or "stuffing balls." Someone had gathered a handful of dressing and rolled it into a baseball-sized circle, baked it, and served it. I had never seen such a delicacy. I thought quickly, *Maybe the cornbread is inside the filling ball.* I broke it open, but all I could see covering half of my plate was bread, more bread. I couldn't believe it. *Haven't they ever heard of serving bread as a side dish? Why do they have to put it all in the dressing? Where is the cornbread? Where is my cornbread?*

I knew at that very moment the difference between stuffing and dressing—filling. Dressing is made with cornbread, and the others are made with bread. I get it. And while I don't agree with it, I have since moved on and have learned to enjoy both. Both are delicious, but just so very different.

After the meal, instead of going to the couch and taking a nap, it was time to shoot the guns in (make sure the guns shoot straight when a bul-let is fired and, if not, adjust them until they do so) and get them ready for deer hunting. There are only two weeks of rifle season where I now live, and they begin the Monday after Thanksgiving. Schools and some offices close for business on the first two days of deer season, ensuring every family can be fed that winter with the deer they harvest. Venison is a huge staple in my area, and there are many ways to make it savory. I, of course, have not been able to master those ways, but many others have. They grill it, marinate it, bake it, sauté it, stew it, and can it. It's amazing. It makes me understand how important shooting in a gun is on the afternoon of Thanksgiving. And that is exactly how I spent my first Thanksgiving afternoon in the North.

Finally my parents arrived that evening, and we took them out for a traditional Thanksgiving meal at a local restaurant. I had yet to cook a turkey—ever—in my whole life, and I certainly didn't want to start on that day. I wanted to spend time with my family and worry as little as possible about food. Actually, I'm terrified of cooking a holiday meal. For one who loves to eat a good meal, I am scared to death to cook one. I am severely insecure when it comes to cooking. And if you add the pressures from a holiday gathering, I become unable to produce anything worth eating. I've been known to completely destroy a grilled cheese sandwich just by forgetting I was cooking one in the first place. I've turned a perfect chicken breast into a small brick and plate-sized hamburger patties into meatballs, all because I tried to cook them. I am easily distracted, and it is just best for me and the safety of my family if I stay out of the kitchen.

So we took my parents to a great local restaurant that had it all—from the turkey to the beets—and we ordered it all. The conversation was wonderful. We discussed the Mississippi State/Ole Miss football game. We talked about everything they saw on their trip, and we cried because they would have to leave. And then I saw my mother about to try the dressing for the very first time. I had not had time to tell her about the difference between stuffing and dressing, but as soon as she took a bite I knew she recognized it. And then she said it, out loud, "Who took the cornbread from this dressing?"

I had never laughed so hard. My husband stared at us both with disbelief as we talked another half hour about the differences between dressing, stuffing, and filling.

The following year we spent Thanksgiving in Mississippi. I'll never forget the first time my husband tasted Southern dressing. His eyes widened and he calmly murmured, "Where's the bread? What's this gritty stuff in the stuffing?"

"That's cornbread, dear," I responded. "Cornbread in the dressing. Isn't it fabulous?"

"Hardly. What's wrong with you Southerners? Don't you'uns know about bread down here?"

"Yes, we do, and we use it appropriately—to sop up our gravy. Can you please pass me more dressing?"

Delta Roasted Turkey

12-15-pound turkey
2 cups red wine
6 whole peppercorns
2 tablespoons parsley
3 sticks butter

4 strips smoked bacon
1½ cups chicken broth
2 bay leaves
1 teaspoon thyme
salt and pepper

Wash turkey and remove giblets, neck, and anything else in it. Dry the bird. Coat it with 1 stick of softened butter and liberally salt and pepper the entire bird. Cut a sheet or pillowcase into a square big enough to wrap the entire turkey. Using a "V" shaped rack and roasting pan, place the cloth over the rack and put 4 strips of smoked bacon on the cloth. Place the turkey breast side down on top of the bacon and fold the cloth up and over the turkey so it is fully covered. In the bottom of the roasting pan, pour red wine, 1 cup chicken broth, peppercorns, bay leaves, parsley, and thyme. Place the turkey into a 500-degree oven and roast for 20 minutes.

In a sauté pan, melt 2 sticks of butter with 1 teaspoon each of salt and pepper and ½ cup chicken broth. After the turkey has roasted 20 minutes, liberally baste the turkey with the butter mixture. Make sure the entire cloth around the bird is saturated. Turn the oven to 300 degrees and continue roasting until a meat thermometer registers 170 degrees in the breast and 180 degrees in the thigh. Baste the turkey every hour with pan juices. If the pan dries, then pour in equal parts red wine and chicken broth. 15-20 minutes before the roasting time is up, remove the cloth and flip the turkey over so that the breast side is up. Brush the breast with melted butter so the skin will crisp and brown. Once the turkey is ready, remove the bird to a warm platter.

Million Dollar Gravy

2 cups juices from turkey pan
2 tablespoons softened butter
salt and pepper to taste

red wine if needed
2 tablespoons all-purpose flour

Strain the juices left in the roasting pan. If necessary, add enough red wine to make at least 2 cups of liquid. Then pour it back into the pan. Place the pan over medium heat and use a wooden spoon to scrape the brown bits from the bottom of the pan. Blend softened butter and all-purpose flour to make a paste. Whisk into roasting pan and bring to a simmer. Continue to whisk until thick. Taste to adjust salt and pepper.

Call Me Southern Cornbread Dressing

I have had long discussions with my cousin and brother-in-law about the fact that our favorite foods should be revered and should only be eaten occasionally. Their favorite is fried chicken, mine is dressing and cranberry sauce. So although it kills us, we will pass it up and eat it only a few times a year because we don't want it to become commonplace. Some people feel the exact opposite, saying "you are going to be dead a long time. You should enjoy your favorite foods at all opportunities." Whichever camp you belong to, this dressing recipe is the best.

3 stalks celery
½ medium yellow onion, chopped
½ medium bell pepper, chopped
3 tablespoons butter
2 teaspoons sage
1 teaspoon poultry seasoning
1 bay leaf
⅛ teaspoon cayenne pepper
5 cups crumbled cornbread
4 cups crumbled saltine cracker crumbs
4½ cups chicken broth
4 beaten eggs

Sauté celery, onions, and bell pepper in butter until translucent. Add sage, poultry seasoning, bay leaf, and cayenne pepper and sauté for 2-3 minutes more. Remove bay leaf. Mix cornbread, cracker crumbs, vegetables, and chicken broth. Stir until well mixed and liquid has absorbed into the cornbread and crackers. At this point, it should be very moist and mushy (close to the consistency of loose oatmeal). Fold in the eggs. Pour into a 9x13 casserole dish. Bake at 350 degrees for 35-45 minutes. Dressing should be set in the middle and golden brown.

Somebody Put Sweet Potatoes in My Orange Cups

8 medium oranges	6 small sweet potatoes
3 tablespoons butter	2 teaspoons vanilla
1 14-ounce can sweetened condensed milk	⅛ teaspoon nutmeg
⅛ teaspoon allspice	⅛ teaspoon cinnamon
zest of one orange	1 cup miniature marshmallows

Remove the top quarter of the oranges and scoop out the flesh with a melon baller or small ice cream scoop. Orange flesh can be eaten, saved for another recipe, or discarded. Peel, cube, and boil potatoes until very tender. While potatoes are still hot, place in a standard mixer with a paddle attachment. Add butter, vanilla, milk, spices, and orange zest and beat on medium speed for 5 minutes. Stop and clean the paddle to remove tough fibers. Continue to beat at medium speed for 3-4 more minutes. Taste and adjust seasonings. Spoon into orange cups and bake at 350 degrees for 20 minutes. Top with marshmallows and return to oven until tops are melted and golden.

This Ain't from a Can Cranberry Sauce

1 cup sugar	1 cup water
juice of 1 orange	1 12-ounce package fresh cranberries
1 tablespoon orange zest	½ cup chopped pecans
1 20-ounce can of crushed pineapple, well drained	

Boil sugar in water until the sugar melts. Add orange juice, cranberries, and orange zest. Boil until the cranberries break, about 5-8 minutes. Let mixture cool to room temperature. Add pecans and pineapple. Chill in refrigerator for at least 3 hours.

Oysters Osceola

2 cups fine cracker crumbs
½ cup chopped green onions
Tabasco to taste
½ cup finely chopped parsley
½ cup melted butter
¾ cup half & half

2 quarts raw oysters, drained
salt and pepper to taste
2 tablespoons Worcestershire sauce
2 tablespoons fresh lemon juice
2 teaspoons paprika

Butter the bottom of a 9x13 casserole dish. Spread 1 cup of cracker crumbs across the bottom of dish. Top with half of the oysters. Sprinkle ¼ cup chopped green onions, ¼ cup parsley, salt, pepper, and Tabasco. Add 1 tablespoon Worcestershire sauce, 1 tablespoon lemon juice, ¼ cup melted butter, and 1 teaspoon paprika. Repeat the layer one more time starting over with the remaining cracker crumbs. After the second layer is completed, make 8 evenly spaced, holes in the top of the casserole with your fingertips. Pour the half & half into the holes equally. Bake at 375 degrees for 30 minutes or until firm.

Asparagus with Shallot Butter

3 ounces pancetta
3 cloves garlic, finely chopped
1 pound asparagus
salt to taste

3 tablespoons butter
2-3 shallots, finely chopped
1½ tablespoons extra virgin olive oil

Cook pancetta in a medium sauté pan until crisp. Remove pancetta with a slotted spoon and set aside. Add butter to pan and sauté garlic and shallots until translucent. Return pancetta to pan and stir to combine. Remove the woody ends of the asparagus and place spears on a rimmed baking sheet. Coat the asparagus in olive oil and season with salt. Roast in a 400-degree oven until asparagus is tender, about 5-7 minutes. Remove asparagus to a serving platter and pour the shallot butter mixture over the asparagus before serving.

Parmesan Mashed Potatoes

10 Russet potatoes, peeled and cubed
2 teaspoons salt plus additional for water
½ cup Hellmann's Mayonnaise
½ cup shredded Parmesan cheese

½ cup milk
1 teaspoon pepper
2 cloves garlic, minced
3 1-teaspoon pats butter,

Boil potatoes in salted water until fork tender and drain. In a standard mixer with a paddle attachment, add milk to the potatoes and whip for 3 minutes on medium. Add salt, pepper, mayonnaise, garlic, and Parmesan and continue to mix until combined. Pour into a 2-quart casserole dish and dot with butter pats. Bake at 350 degrees for 30 minutes.

He's Gone Hunting Horseradish Mashed Potatoes

10 Russet potatoes, peeled and cubed
2 teaspoons salt plus additional for water
½ cup sour cream

½ cup milk or half & half
1 teaspoon pepper
3 teaspoons prepared horseradish

Boil potatoes in salted water until fork tender. Drain and place in a stand mixer fitted with a paddle attachment. Add milk or half & half. Beat for 3 minutes on medium speed. Add salt, pepper, sour cream, and horseradish. Continue to beat until all are combined. Serve while still warm.

Both potato recipes can be prepared with a potato masher or hand blender.

The Girls Stayed Home Grand Mimosas

1 750-ml bottle chilled Champagne or sparkling wine   2 cups chilled fresh orange juice
¼ to ½ cup orange liqueur

Stir together and serve immediately.

Conclusion
LIFE LESSONS

Southern Conclusions, n.: The final word, the end of a conversation or story . . . or when your escort to the ball has to break up the catfight you're in over whether you are wearing diamonds or rhinestones.

The Mississippi Delta is a place that has been represented in great literature and has even been the main character of a few films. It is also the place where two little girls formed a friendship that would span almost four decades. This friendship would be filled with Florida vacations, prank calls, baby and bridal showers, tailgating, cotillions, midnight drive-bys of an ex-boyfriend's house, weddings, funerals, and even cross-country moves.

Elizabeth has offered me some very helpful tips along the way that I think will help you too: There are stores where you can get name-brand items but don't have to pay name-brand prices; you don't have to date losers if you don't want to; a friend is not the person who buys you the biggest gift (although that can change depending on the gift); always try to be positive about every situation; know how to speak well of people (even your enemies); don't be that girl who drinks too much at the party and turns from debutante to stripper; and for goodness' sake, never ever let a guest see you with your silver not polished.

The last bit of advice I remember Elizabeth giving me was, "Susanne, don't even think about moving north. They will eat you alive. I heard they don't even use cornbread in their dressing. You will go nuts." Was she right? Well, it all depends on the day.

Somebody stole the CORNBREAD

Index of Recipes
By Category

Appetizers, Soups, & Dips

Desserts

Bye-Bye Resolutions Banana Pudding, 59
Chocolate Chip Bundt Cake, 74
Chocolate Covered Strawberries, 87
Chocolate Snowballs, 87
Coconut Glop Cake, 75
Grandmother's Buttermilk Cake, 59
Peanut Butter Bars, 40
Petite Tarts with Lime or Chocolate, 105

Drinks

Big Will's Bloody Mary, 39
French Pregtinis, 101
Missing Bride's Mojitos, 27
The Girls Stayed Home Grand Mimosas, 117

Sandwiches & Main Courses

Sauces

Side Dishes and Breads

Acknowledgments
SPECIAL THANKS

from Elizabeth

- Momma and Daddy, thank you for always making me feel like just breathing was enough. Your unconditional love made all the difference in who I am today.
- Grandmother and the rest of my family, I will always be grateful for the Southern sensibility you so generously gave me.
- William, I could not be more proud of you.
- Amanda, you are the best assistant money can't buy. Aren't you sick of me yet?
- Amanda, Cordelia, Jill, Jincy, Marsha, Camile, Holly, Melissa, and Mary Elizabeth, even though I am sure you were tired of listening, thank you for not yawning.
- Deloris and Bird, thank you for teaching me to cook food that really makes a difference.
- Carol, your support and encouragement have changed the course of my life. I will be forever grateful.
- Caroline, without your perfect eye and persistence, this book would be nothing.
- Babo, Julie, and the rest of Luke's family, thank you for believing this could happen.
- Viking Cooking School and Beth, thank you for allowing me to work in a place that was built on nothing but a dream. Always reminding me that anything is possible.
- Beth and Jon, thank you for loving this book as much as we did.
- Clark Jewelry, McCartys Pottery, and Nan Sanders, thank you for not hanging up the phone every time you all heard "All I need are are just a few things." Your pieces made the food come alive.

from Susanne

- To Mama, I love you so much! My heart swells with love each time I watch you with Carter. You are a wonderful grandmother. I only wish we lived closer so we could see you more often. We all love you and miss you each day we are apart.
- To my late father, I was lucky enough to have a wonderful man as a role model in my life. He was witty, kind and Christian . . . who could ask for anything more in a father? I was a truly blessed child.
- To Melanie, Christie, and my other Southern friends, thank you for so many great memories, for keeping me grounded, and for not yelling at me when I don't keep in touch like I should.
- To Lindsey, Sherry, and my other Northern friends, I'm so thankful to have met so many wonderful people who have taught me the Northern ropes and have truly become very dear friends to me and my family.
- To all of my in-laws (and some outlaws), I love you all! You are wonderful to me. You welcomed me with open arms and have always made me feel like a part of your family.
- To the rest of my family, I love each and every one of you. Yes, you.
- To Sarah, a new friend and great photographer. You handled a crazy Southern woman in a crisis with ease . . . a rare talent. Thank you!

Notes
AND RECIPES

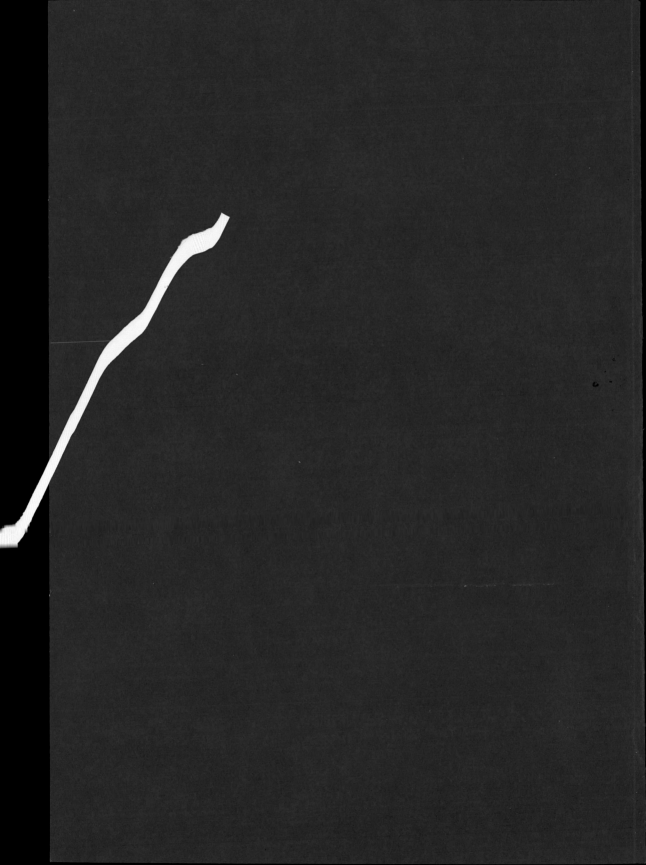